Table Of Contents

Kindle Controls

Using your Kindle Paperwhite is simple. You only need to learn a few simple steps to control it.

Power Button: You can turn your Kindle Paperwhite on by pressing the Power button, located on the top edge of your Kindle Paperwhite. Turning the device off is easy – press and hold the power button for 9 seconds after which the Power Dialog Box will appear - simply tap the Screen Off prompt.

The Kindle will enter sleep mode automatically after a few minutes of inactivity. A static screensaver will be displayed while under Sleep Mode. This Static Screensaver does not use battery power.

The device can be put into Sleep Mode by pressing and releasing the Power Button. Follow the same steps to wake up your Kindle.

In the event that your Kindle is non-responsive, you can restart the device by holding down the power button for 9 seconds. The Power Dialog box will be displayed, and you can select the restart prompt. If the Power Dialog box does not appear, press and hold the Power Button until the LED light stops blinking – this usually takes 15 seconds.

Micro-USB/Power Port: Use the USD cable that comes with your Kindle device to connect it to a computer for charging or file transferring.

You can also charge your Kindle Paperwhite using a power outlet and the USB cable with an Amazon 5W charger which is sold separately. A lightning bolt icon will be displayed next to the battery status indicator located at the top of the Home screen when the device is charging. The indicator light will be orange while the battery is charging and will turn green when fully charged.

Using the Amazon 5W charger should take less than two hours to fully charge your Kindle. Charging from a computer or using a generic adapter should take less than three hours, but it is important to understand that this depends on the quality of the hardware being used.

It is possible to use your Kindle while it is connected to your computer via the USB cable and charging. Unmount or eject the device so that it exits USB drive mode. In Windows, you can do this by right-clicking the 'Safely Remove Hardware' icon in the task bar and following the onscreen instructions to safely remove your device. In Mac OS X, click the eject button that is next to the Kindle in the Finder window or drag it from the desktop into trash. Once done, your Kindle will exit USB Drive Mode, but remain charging.

If the charge indicator light on the bottom of the device does not come on, check the USB cable and ensure that it is properly connected to both the device and the USB port of your computer. Try using a different USB port or power outlet if the problem persists.

Note: Older computers and keyboards may have low-powered USB ports that may not provide enough power for your Kindle to charge.

Status Indicators

The indicators at the top of the Home Screen keep you informed about the status of your Kindle Paperwhite. Tap the top of the screen to display these toolbars when you're in the middle of a book or a document.

Wireless Status Indicators

Thanks to Amazon Whispernet service, you can have content delivered to your Kindle device wherever and whenever you need to. The Kindle Paperwhite uses its built-in Wi-Fi capability to connect to Whispernet. Some models also provide free cellular network connectivity to Whispernet. The bars on the Wi-Fi or Cellular Network Status Indicators, show the strength of the signal.

Indicates that the device is connected to Whispernet using Wi-Fi.

 Indicates that the Kindle is connected to Whispernet through a cellular network. The icon to the left of the Signal-Strength Bars icon indicates what type of cellular network the device is connected to. (Applies to Kindle Wi-Fi + Cellular.)

Indicates that your Kindle Paperwhite is in Airplane Mode. Wireless and Bluetooth connectivity will be turned off while in Airplane Mode.

Battery Status Indicator

This indicator shows the remaining battery life of the device. When your Kindle is being charged, a lightning bolt will appear within the battery icon.

Note: Weak wireless signals increase power consumption.

Audio Indicators

�֎ Indicates that your Kindle device is searching for audio devices under Pairing Mode or that a Bluetooth audio device is currently paired with it.

◀) Indicates that a Bluetooth audio device or VoiceView screen reader is connected or playing.

Activity Indicator

↺ Appears at the top left corner of your Home screen. It indicates that the device is scanning for a network or connecting to one, downloading content, syncing, checking for new items, searching for items, opening a PDF file or loading a web page.

Parental Controls Indicator

🔒 Indicates that Parental Controls are enabled on your device. Parental Controls are enabled when you turn them on or when a Kindle FreeTime (Kindle for Kids in the UK) profile is active.

Keyboard

The Onscreen Keyboard on your Kindle Paperwhite automatically displays at the bottom of the screen when you tap within a text box or any other action that requires a keyboard. Tap the appropriate keys to make a selection. Word suggestions will appear above the keyboard as you type. Simply tap a word to select it.

Tips:

• Click the Number key to select numbers or symbols.

• Return to the standard keyboard by clicking the letter key.

• Uppercase letters can be created by clicking the shift key. Click shift twice to enter all-cap mode. Exit all-cap by tapping the shift key once.

• Different languages can be accessed by clicking the Quick Actions icon and selecting all settings. Select Language and Dictionaries, then Keyboards to access your chosen language.

• Special characters and diacritics can be accessed by selecting and holding the base letters' key. Press and hold the 'e' key to display é, è, or ê.

• A Globe key will appear on your keyboard when you use multiple languages. Tap the Globe key to select different keyboards.

Set Up and Charge

Setting up of your Kindle Paperwhite takes only a few easy steps:

- First select the preferred device language.
- Then Connect the Kindle Paperwhite to a wireless network.
- Register your Kindle Paperwhite on your Amazon account.
- Link your Kindle Paperwhite to your social network accounts. (This is optional)

Register or Deregister Kindle Paperwhite

You can buy, download or deliver content to your device once you Register it to your Amazon account. You can deregister if your device is registered to the wrong account or if you want to transfer ownership.

You must connect wirelessly and register the device to an Amazon account in order to buy and download content. Once registered, you can download compatible purchases from other devices that are registered to the same account.

Note: A Kindle devices received as a gift may need to be deregistered before registering to your Amazon account.

Registering Your Kindle

1. On the toolbar tap the **Quick Action** icon ⚙ and then tap **All Settings.**
2. Select **My Account**.

3. Click the Amazon account you would like to use on your Kindle Paperwhite device:

- **To use an existing Amazon account**: Tap that specific option while proceeding through the setup process and enter your Amazon account details. Once the registration is complete, your name will appear as the Registered User.
- **To use a new Amazon account**: Tap that specific option and follow the setup steps to create a new Amazon account and register your device under that account.

At time of enabling your Sign in Approval, you will need to enter your passcode. This will prompt a security code to be sent to your phone and is a mandatory action to register the device.

Deregister Your Kindle

Follow the steps below to deregister your Kindle from your Amazon account on your device or from a computer.

Important: Once you deregister your Kindle Paperwhite from your Amazon account, you will not be able to access your Amazon account's stored content library.

In order to deregister your Kindle Paperwhite, you must first connect to a wireless network.

1. On the toolbar tap **Quick Action** icon and then tap **All Settings**.
2. Select **My account**.
3. Tap **Deregister Device**, and then confirm by tapping **Deregister** again. Once you have deregistered your device, you can register it to a new Amazon account.
   Note: Deregistering can also be done via the link Manage Your Content and Devices (https://www.amazon.com/mycd).

Connect Wirelessly

Connect to Wi-Fi

Connecting to a Wi-Fi network enables you to buy and download content, sync to receive items or navigate to the last page read.

Connecting to a Wi-Fi Network:

1. On the toolbar tap the **Quick Actions** icon 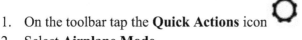 , then tap **All Settings**.
2. Select **Wireless** or **Wi-Fi & Bluetooth**.
3. Below **Wi-Fi Networks**, select a **network** to connect. If a lock icon is displayed, you will require a network password.
    *   **For Wi-Fi networks and routers that support WPS (Wi-Fi Protected Setup):** If WPS is supported, you Kindle will detect that. Proceed by tapping **WPS** from the Wi-Fi Password Required screen and connect by pressing the WPS Association button on your router.
    *   **For networks that don't support WPS:** Simply enter the password for the Wi-Fi network. Contact the individual who set up the network if you don't know the password.

Once you connect to a particular Wi-Fi network, your Kindle will automatically connect to that network whenever it is in range. When there are more than one familiar networks in range, your Kindle Paperwhite will connect to the network that was used most recently.

Note: On Kindle devices that include 3G/4G coverage, 3G/4G coverage will be disabled automatically when you connect to a Wi-Fi network.

Turn Off Wireless (Turn On Airplane Mode)

Save battery power by disabling 3G and Wi-Fi network connections when not in use.

Note: Browsing the web or purchasing, downloading or syncing Kindle books and periodicals is disabled while the wireless connection is turned off.

1. On the toolbar tap the **Quick Actions** icon .
2. Select **Airplane Mode**.

Add a Wi-Fi Network Manually

If the Wi-Fi network you are trying to connect to doesn't appear, add the Wi-Fi network manually.

Ensure that you are within range of the network that you want to connect to. Enter the name and password as required.

1. On the toolbar tap the **Quick Actions** icon ⚙ , and then tap **All Settings**.
2. Select **Wireless** to view the list of Wi-Fi networks in range.
3. Select **Other**.
4. Use the onscreen keyboard to enter the **Network Name**.
5. If a password is required, select the **Password** box and then enter the Wi-Fi password.
6. Finally, select **Connect**.

Tips:

Sometimes, you may forget your network password. If this occurs, check your router and there may be a sticker underneath displaying the default password. • For more information on deleting your saved Wi-Fi passwords, see the managing your saved Wi-Fi passwords section. • Your Kindle Paperwhite does not support connection to ad hoc (or peer-to-peer) Wi-Fi networks. • You can attempt to resolve connectivity issues by turning Airplane Mode on and off. • If difficulties persist, we recommended contacting the Network Administrator or Internet Service Provider responsible for maintenance of the network you are trying to access.

Managing your saved Wi-Fi passwords

You are given the option to save your Wi-Fi password to Amazon at the time of connecting to a Wi-Fi network. After saving the password, Amazon can configure your compatible devices so that you will not need to re-enter your Wi-Fi passwords for each device. Your Wi-Fi passwords will be sent via a secured connection and encrypted on an Amazon server. To connect compatible devices, Amazon may use your Wi-Fi passwords. Amazon will not share your details with any third party without your permission, in accordance with the Amazon.com Privacy Notice.

You will need to opt out of the Save Password feature when you enter your network password.

You will need to complete the Wi-Fi setup process again to change your Wi-Fi password in the future. Your updated Wi-Fi password will be automatically saved to Amazon (if you have chosen not to opt out of this feature) after reconnection to your Wi-Fi network.

To delete stored Wi-fi passwords, follow the below steps:

1. Select the Quick Actions icon on the toolbar and then tap All Settings.
2. From the Settings page, select Wi-Fi & Bluetooth and then select Delete Wi-Fi Passwords.
3. Double click Delete to confirm it.

Connecting to 3G

If you have disabled wireless on your device, turn it back on to connect to a 3G network to purchase and download content, connect to the Cloud and sync or return to the most recent page read.

If 3G is enabled, connecting to a Wi-Fi network will automatically turn off 3G coverage. Your Kindle Paperwhite will switch back to 3G coverage when you disconnect from a Wi-Fi network or when you move out of Wi-Fi range.

Wireless connectivity is automatic for Kindle models that include free 3G free of monthly fees or annual contracts. If your Kindle Paperwhite is connected wirelessly by 3G you will see a 3G network indicator: 3G, EDGE or GPRS in the upper right corner of your screen.

Note: Access to Amazon.com or Wikipedia via the experimental Web Browser is only available when connected by 3G. Unrestricted access can be gained by connecting to a Wi-Fi network.

1. Select the **Quick Actions** icon ⬡ if 3G is turned off.
2. Select **Airplane Mode**.

About 3G Coverage

3G Kindle Paperwhite is equipped with Wi-Fi as well as built-in free 3G wireless connectivity with coverage in over 100 countries and territories. If 3G is not available at your current location, select Wi-Fi.

Note: Downloaded content should be available on your Kindle within 60 seconds. However, download time is dependent on your Wi-Fi network settings, 3G or EDGE/GPRS coverage, signal strength and the size of the file you are downloading.

Visit 3G Coverage Map (http://client0.cellmaps.com/viewer.html?cov=1) to check the 3G coverage in your area.

Important Information about the Coverage Map

Actual coverage might be substantially different from what is displayed on the map. Coverage may also be affected by terrain, weather, foliage, buildings and other obstructions, signal strength and other factors. Therefore, coverage is not guaranteed by Amazon.

VoiceView Screen Reader

You can navigate your Kindle using special gestures and receive voice guidance when you interact with items on the screen and hear audio readings of books with VoiceView Screen Reader. When setting up your Kindle, pair a Bluetooth audio device for use with the VoiceView screen reader. Ensure that you read all instructions before starting the setup and reference the instructions when needed. You will receive no audio announcements or feedback until the last step.

1. Turn your Kindle **On** by pressing the **Power** button once.
2. Wait 45 seconds.
3. Set your Bluetooth audio device into pairing mode.
4. Press and hold the **Power** button for 9 seconds.
5. Place two fingers on the screen for 1 second. Wait up to 2 minutes to hear audio.
6. Place two fingers on the screen once you hear audio from your Bluetooth device

Troubleshooting: If after 2 minutes of completing step 5, you do not hear audio from your Bluetooth device, first ensure that Bluetooth audio device is in pairing mode. Repeat steps 4 and 5. The VoiceView tutorial will begin once your audio device is connected and VoiceView is enabled for the first time.

You will need to complete the setup by connecting to a wireless network and registering your Kindle Paperwhite. Before turning on VoiceView after the setup, ensure your Bluetooth audio device is on before waking your Kindle from sleep mode using the **Power** button. Hold down the Kindle **Power** button for 9 seconds. Then hold two fingers on the screen. VoiceView audio should resume after 6 seconds.

It is possible to turn VoiceView on and off via Settings. Tap the **Quick Actions** icon on the toolbar and then tap **All Settings** to manage

VoiceView screen reader settings. On the **Settings** page, tap **Accessibility**. If VoiceView is currently enabled, the All Settings option in Quick Actions will appear as VoiceView Settings.

Special Offers and Sponsored Screensavers

Periodically, you will be invited to receive Special Offers and Sponsored Screensavers for your Kindle Paperwhite. Special Offers will display only on the Home screen or screensaver—never within a book. Keep in mind that Special Offers and Sponsored Screensavers are only available for selected countries and may not be available in your region.

Screensaver

A Special Offer will displayed on your screensaver when your device is in sleep mode. To see more details about the offer, wake up your Kindle Paperwhite and select **Tap for Details.** You can unlock your Kindle Paperwhite without viewing the offer details by swiping your finger down the screen to unlock.

Special Offer banners

Special Offer banners will appear at the bottom of your Home screen. You can view the details by tapping the **banner** and following the below steps:

1. Click the Home icon and then tap the Menu icon.
2. Select View Special Offers.
3. Select available offers to view additional details.

If you purchase a Special Offer when your Kindle Paperwhite is offline your order will be queued and processed when you next connect to a network. You can also manage Special Offers by selecting the Quick Actions icon on the toolbar and then selecting All Settings, then My Account and tapping Special Offers.

Change Your Kindle E-Reader Device Language

Selecting the default language will update your Kindle Paperwhite menus, keyboard and its default dictionary.

Your Kindle Paperwhite default device language can be set to the following languages: English (U.S., UK), German, French (France, Canada), Italian,

Spanish (Spain, Mexico, Argentina, Chile and Colombia), Portuguese (Brazil), Japanese, Chinese (Simplified), Russian, or Dutch.

Kindle Paperwhite menus, keyboard, and default dictionary will update automatically when a new language is selected. Note that the User Guide and any other downloaded content will remain in the original language.

Note: Changing the language on your Kindle device, will result in the corresponding language dictionary and keyboard being automatically downloaded to your device when connected to Wi-Fi where available. Follow the steps below to change your language settings:

1. Tap the **Quick Actions** icon ⚙ on the toolbar, followed by **All Settings**.
2. Tap **Language and Dictionaries**. Then select from the following options:
   - **Language** – choose an alternate language for your Kindle.
   - **Keyboard** - choose the region-specific layout for your keyboard.
   - **Dictionaries** - choose the default language dictionary.

Charge Your Kindle E-Reader

It takes four to six hours to fully charge your Kindle using the supplied USB cable. If you use an alternate charging device it may take longer depending on the capability and quality of the hardware that you use.

Tip: Conserve battery life by placing your Kindle Paperwhite into Sleep Mode when not in use.

Note: Your Kindle Paperwhite can be charged from a power outlet using a power adapter that is compatible with the USB cable. It should not take more than four hours to charge your device using a Kindle branded power adapter.

You can charge your Kindle by connecting the supplied USB cable to a computer or to a compatible power adapter which is connected to a power outlet.

A lightning bolt will appear within the battery icon 🔋 at the top of the **Home** screen when your Kindle Paperwhite is charging.

The indicator light that is built into the power button on the top right side of your Kindle Paperwhite will turn orange while charging. If the light doesn't appear, check your cables are correctly inserted.

The Kindle Paperwhite Leather Charging cover is equipped with a built-in battery designed to extend the reading time of your device in between charges. The cover connects to the device without the need for an additional power adapter.

Note: The cover only charges when attached to the Kindle using its external charging port.

Using Your Kindle

Turn your Kindle On / Off	Turn your Kindle on by pressing and holding the Power button for seven seconds. To turn it off, tap Screen Off in the prompt box that appears.
Turn pages	Turn pages by swiping your finger in the direction you want to turn the page. You can also click the left or right side of the screen.
Make a selection	From the Home screen, tap the screen to access options or open a book. While reading a book, you can access the dictionary, X-Ray (if available), and translation by long tapping a word. You can highlight text by selecting more than five words at a time. In order to access the Reading Toolbar, tap the top of the screen.
Set the screen orientation	While reading: 1. Reading Toolbar can be accessed by tapping the top of the screen.

2. Tap the **Display Settings** icon (Aa). Then tap the **Page** tab.
3. Select **Portrait Mode** or **Landscape Mode** listed under **Orientation**.

Panel View Navigation   You can magnify comic and graphic novel panels with Panel View to read them fully. Double tap on the top of the screen to enter Panel View while reading. You can exit Panel View by double tapping the screen again.

Navigate Your Kindle E-Reader Home Screen

You can manage and organize your Kindle content on the Home screen with the instructions below.

Toolbars

Standard Toolbars

- **Accessing the Home screen**: Tap the **Home**   icon.

- **Returning to the previous screen**: Tap the **Back**   icon.
- **Accessing screen light controls, Airplane Mode, Bluetooth, Sync My Kindle, and All Settings.**: Tap the **Quick Action**   icon.
  Screen Light: Click to adjust screen light controls with the following steps:
    - Drag your finger along the slider until you reach the desired setting.
    - To select a specific setting touch that section of the slider.
    - Then select the icon to use a higher light setting.
    - Next, you can preselect the icon to use a lower light setting.
    - Press and hold the icon to select the maximum brightness setting.

- You can also press and hold the icon to choose the minimum setting as well.

Airplane Mode: By enabling this feature, your Wireless and Bluetooth connectivity will be disabled.

Bluetooth: Activate Bluetooth by selecting the Bluetooth feature.

Sync My Kindle: Use this to synchronize your Kindle Paperwhite with your other supported devices.

All Settings: Access All Settings by selecting the Menu Icon. Use this feature to further customize your Kindle Paperwhite.

- **Accessing Goodreads on Kindle**: Tap the **Goodreads** g icon to proceed to Goodreads.

    Note: You may be prompted to sign in to Goodreads or to create a new account if you have not already done so.

- **Accessing Kindle Store**: Tap the **Store** store icon.
- **Searching for content** – You can search for content by tapping the **Search** icon and then entering your search terms. To exit, tap outside of the Search bar.
- **Menu**: The menu icon displays a list of options including: My Library, My Reading Lists, Kindle Store, Audible Store, Goodreads, Kindle FreeTime (Kindle for Kids in the UK), Vocabulary Builder, Experimental Browser, Settings, View Special Offers (Kindle with Special Offers devices only) and Create New Collection.

    Further menu options may include Shop Kindle Store, Shop Audible Store, Vocabulary Builder, Settings, Notes, About This Book, About the Author, Sync to Furthest Page Read and Word Wise at the time of reading a book.

Reading Toolbars

Tap the top of your screen to access the secondary toolbar when you're reading a book.

Go To: The Contents page of the book you are reading including the Beginning and Title Chapters are displayed on the Contents Tab. You can navigate through your book by clicking page or chapter options. Notes and highlights can be accessed by tapping the Notes prompt. Select the corresponding options under the Notes prompt to view popular highlights.

X-Ray: Use the X-Ray feature to explore the "Bones of the Book" – see passages in the book that mention specific ideas, characters, historical figures, places, topics, terms, etc., - view notable clips and images organized on a timeline like a deck of cards. Easily view the clips and images in one place, quickly. The X-Ray option will not appear if the feature is unavailable for a particular book.

Display Settings (Aa): Tapping this displays font and text options for your Kindle book such as font, font size, bold, line spacing, margins, screen orientation and alignment. It also allows you to choose your preferred Reading Progress tracking option.

Share: Share your views with your friends using Goodreads on Kindle and other social networks by selecting the Share tab.

Bookmarks: You can add or delete a bookmark on the current page and view previously added bookmarks by tapping the Bookmark icon. The Bookmark icon will turn from White to Black when you are on a bookmarked page. A preview pane will appear when you tap a bookmark on the list. You can navigate to the selected page by tapping the preview pane. Simply tap outside of the bookmark dropdown to exit the Bookmark feature.

Reading Navigation Toolbars

Tap the top of the screen while reading to access the Reading Navigation toolbar. The Reading Navigation toolbar shows the name of the chapter (if available), reading progress, and options to help you explore your book.

Switch to Listening: A headphone icon will appear on the bottom right of the screen when you access the Reading Navigation toolbar if the book you are reading has an Audiobook version. Tap the Headphone icon to listen to the audiobook version.

Periodical Toolbar: Toolbars are configured specifically for periodicals. Tap the top of the screen to display the toolbar.

Periodical Home: Tap to access highlights of each particular issue.

Sections and Articles: Tapping this will display a hierarchical list of sections and articles in a newspaper or a magazine. Note: this option is not available for blogs.

There will be a secondary toolbar if you are reading a periodical and you are on the article detail page. Its options include:

Display Settings (Aa): Tapping this will show font and text options for your periodicals, including font, font size, bold, line spacing, margins, screen orientation and alignment. Choose your preferred Reading Progress tracking option here.

Clip This Article: Tapping this will clip an article to the My Clippings file. The My Clippings file can be found in your library. It stores notes, bookmarks, highlights and clipped articles.

Managing your Kindle Library

- Swipe the screen to go to the next or previous page to easily navigate your library. You can also tap the page number control which is located in the bottom right of the screen. The two numbers shown indicate the current page you are on, and the number of pages in the document. You can manually enter a number to instantly navigate to that page.
- **View Kindle content in the Cloud** – You can view all the content purchased through the Kindle store by tapping the **All** tab. You can download your content from the Cloud when you're connected to a wireless network.
  - o **Note:** Already downloaded content with have a checkmark display on the cover.

- **View Kindle content stored on your device** – Tapping the **Downloaded** tab shows the titles you've started to read along with the percentage read on the cover. Titles you have not yet read will show 'new' on their cover.
- **Open your content** – You can open a book by tapping on its title. If the title that you click is not already on your device, it will automatically download if your Kindle is connected to a wireless network.
- **Periodicals**
  Newspapers and magazines are categorized by name and stored in folders . You can select all to view all the periodicals that you have stored in the Cloud or Downloaded to view single issues. Audible Periodicals are not stored in folders and will appear as single titles in your library. Issues that are more than eight issues old are automatically deleted to free up space for new content. Newspapers that are more than 14 issues old and magazines that are more than 40 issues old will be automatically deleted from the Cloud as well. "Expiring" next to an issue indicates that is soon to be deleted. You can press and hold on a

18

periodical folder to view the following options: Download Latest Issue and Remove All Back Issues. Keep in mind that Audible periodicals do not expire and will remain on your device and backed up to the Cloud.

Tap the menu icon located on the periodical's cover to view more options when in Grid view or on the right side of the screen when in List view. Options include: Add to Home, Add to Collection and Go to First Page, Go to Sections & Articles, Search This Issue, Keep This Issue, View Notes & Marks, View Back Issues, and Delete this Issue. By pressing and holding on the name or cover of the issue, you can also view these options.

To save a copy of an issue on your device, there are the two ways:

First tap Downloaded on your library screen. Tap the Menu icon located on the issue's cover when in Grid view or on the right side of the screen when in List view. Select Keep This Issue. Press and hold the name or cover of the issue to also view this option. You will need to tap the Menu icon from within the issue to Keep This Issue.

Go to www.amazon.com/devicesupport, to access all your back issues, regardless of age. You can also access the Manage Your Content and Devices page from this link.

- **Filter your content** – Filter your content by tapping the left drop-down menu in the upper right corner of the screen (below the Search bar). Then tap **All**, **Books**, **Periodicals**, **Docs**, or **Collections** to filter.
- **Panel View Navigation** – Tap a comic or manga title to open it. Double tap the screen. Proceed to Display Settings to activate Panel View Navigation. Click on 'X' at the top right to exit Panel View.

Turn Automatic Book Updates On or Off

You can select whether to receive automatic updates for your Kindle books. If you enable this setting, your downloaded content will receive the latest updated version with corrections and improvements where available.

It is up to the user to ensure your Kindle device and reading apps have Annotations Backup or Whispersync for books activated to preserve your reading progress, bookmarks, notes, highlights and annotations across different versions of books.

Here is the process to enable or disable Automatic Book Updates:

1. Go to <u>Manage Your Content and Devices</u> (<u>https://www.amazon.com/mycd</u>).
2. Select the **Settings** tab.
3. Select **on** or **off** under **Automatic Book Update**.

Note: After selecting **off**, you will no longer receive automatic book updates, however an author or publisher can send you request via email to do so.

Clear the Furthest Page Read

The Furthest Page Read feature is an effective tool that allows you to stop reading your book or periodical and pick up where you left off on another Fire tablet, Kindle e-reader or Kindle reading app that is registered to the same Amazon account.

We recommend clearing the furthest page read after completing your book or periodical to prevent your title from opening at the last page on other devices that are registered to the same account.

Here are the processes to clear the furthest page read for a title:

1. Go to <u>Manage Your Content and Devices</u> (<u>https://www.amazon.com/mycd</u>).
2. Locate the correct title on the **Your Content** tab.
3. Click the **Actions** button.
4. Select the **Clear Furthest Page Read** button to confirm.

When you open the title the next time on your device of choice, the page that opens will become the new furthest page read. This function will sync across all devices registered on the same account.

Change the Home Screen View

Change the layout of your Kindle Paperwhite Home screen to either List or Grid view.

- Home Screen View shows My Library, My Reading Lists and Recommendations.
- List or Grid view displays Kindle content in your Kindle Library.

In order to change your Kindle home screen:

1. Tap the **Quick Action** icon. Then tap **All Settings**
2. Tap **Device Options**.

3. Tap **Advanced Options** and then slide the toggle underneath **Home Screen View** to **Off**.

Adjust the Screen Light

You can maintain optimal reading conditions in bright or dark surroundings with your Kindle's adjustable screen light while reading.

Tap the top of the screen to bring up the toolbar and then tap the Quick Actions icon in order to adjust the screen brightness while reading.

- You can adjust the brightness by sliding your finger along or by tapping the scale to set to the desired setting.
   - o **Tip:** Use a lower setting for surroundings with low lighting and a higher setting if you in a bright lighting.

- To set the light to minimum brightness press and hold the ☀ symbol. Similarly, you can set the light to maximum brightness by pressing and holding the ☀ symbol. On Kindle Paperwhite, tap **Max** to set the light to maximum brightness with a single tap.
   - **Note:** Even while set to the lowest setting, the screen light is not completely off.

- On Kindle Paperwhite, tapping **Auto Brightness** will automatically adjust the screen light. The screen light matches the brightness of your surroundings when **Auto Brightness** is turned on. When you adjust the slider, the **Auto Brightness** feature will use that particular adjustment in the future.
   - **Tip:** When reading with your Kindle in the dark, turning on **Nightlight** will gradually reduce the screen brightness to help your eyes adjust to the dark. You can use the Nightlife feature by, tapping the **Quick Action** ⚙ icon, and then selecting **All Settings > Device Options > Screen Light**.

Tap Zones

Effortlessly turn pages in a book or a periodical by using your Kindle's EasyReach feature while holding the device with only one hand. You can navigate to the next page by tapping almost anywhere in the display area. Go to the previous page by tapping the left side of the screen, move forward by tapping the right of the screen. The tap zones of the EasyReach feature will vary depending on whether your Kindle is in portrait or landscape mode. Screen orientation can be changed by tapping the top of the screen to bring up the toolbars and then tapping Display Settings (Aa). Tap the Page tab and select your desired orientation on the Display Settings dialog.

You can also change pages by swiping your finger across the screen. Swipe your finger to the right to proceed to the next page. Swipe your finger to the left to return to the previous page. It's also possible to turn pages using the controls at the side of your screen.

Customizing your text display

There is a quick way to adjust the appearance of books and periodicals. At the time of reading, tap the top of the screen to show the toolbars. After that, tap the Display Settings icon (Aa) to access settings. A dialog box will appear that displays three tabs including; Font, Page, and Reading Settings.

Tap the Font tab to:

• Select from a list of available fonts. You also have the option to access the publisher font, embedded by the publisher.

• Drag your finger along the slider or tap the plus or minus sign to increase or decrease font size. To zoom, pinch two fingers together on the screen while reading.

• Bold and adjust font up to five levels by dragging your finger along the slider or tapping the plus or minus signs.

Tap the Page tab to:

• Adjust the spacing between lines.

• Increase or decrease margin size.

• Select portrait or landscape screen orientation.

• Change text alignment between justified and left justified.

Tap the Reading Settings tab to:

• Select your preferred reading progress tracking option.

• Select whether or not to show the clock.

Display settings are device specific, meaning any changes you make to these settings will apply to all books you read on your Kindle. Note that your Kindle also applies kerning and will optimize layout for large fonts and automatically optimize line spacing for faster, easier reading across all fonts.

Cloud Collections on Kindle E-Readers

The content on your Kindle can be organized into custom categories that will be stored in the Cloud by using Cloud Collections.

With Cloud Collections, you can organize the content on your Kindle device into customized categories. These categories will be stored in the Cloud. Your collections will be synced between other devices as well as reading apps (that support Cloud Collections) that are registered under the same Amazon account. Each collection can contain as many books and personal documents as you wish. The same item can also be added to more than one collection. You cannot add Audible content to collections.

To create a new collection:

1. Tap **My Library** on the Home screen, then tap **Menu.** Then tap **Create New Collection**.
2. Name your collection and tap **OK.** Items on your Kindle that can be added to a collection will appear in the form of a list.
3. Select items you would like to add to the collection by tapping the checkboxes next to their titles.
4. When you have finished selecting items, tap **Done.** The created collection will appear on the **Home** screen.

Follow these instructions to edit or delete a collection:
1. Press and hold the collection title from **Home**.
2. Tap to **Add/Remove Items**, **Rename**, **Remove from Device** or **Delete**.

Important:

- When you delete a collection that was created on a device or Kindle reading app that supports Cloud Collections, it will be deleted from the Cloud as well as from other devices registered under the same Amazon account.
- When you delete a collection that has been imported from a device or a reading app that does NOT support Cloud Collections, the original collection on other devices or Kindle reading apps will not be affected.
- When a collection is deleted, any of the content that is stored in your Kindle Library will NOT be deleted. Items that belonged to a deleted collection will appear on the **Home** screen when you sort items by **Collections**.

View and Manage Your Cloud Collections

Tailor how you view and access collections on your Kindle by categorizing items on your **Home** screen.

Follow these instructions in order to filter items on your **Home** screen:

1. Select **My Library** from **Home**. Use the left drop down menu in the upper right corner of your screen (below the Search bar) to view your options: only **Books, Periodicals, Docs**, or **Collections** will appear.
2. You can see your collections by tapping **Collections.**

All the collections that have been downloaded to your Kindle will appear in your All Items, Books, Comics, Periodicals and Docs views. You can download a collection by tapping the Menu icon on the collections cover when the device is on grid mode or on the right side of your screen when the device is in list view. Proceed by selecting Add to Device. This option can also be viewed by pressing and holding a collection's cover or its name if the device is in list mode. This setting is device-specific and will not be saved when you deregister your Kindle. In order to remove a collection, tap the Menu icon on a collection's cover under grid mode or on the right side of the screen under list mode. Proceed by selecting Remove from Device. It's also possible to view this option by pressing and holding on a collection's cover or title.

Family Library on Kindle

You can share Kindle books with members of your Amazon Household using Family Library. Link Amazon accounts to create an Amazon Household.

24

Using the Cloud tab on your Kindle device, find content that has been shared through Family Library. Filter by My Books or Shared Books in order to choose the content you are viewing.

Creating an Amazon Household from Your Kindle E-Reader

In order to share content through Family Library, both adults will need to provide authorization for each other to use the registered payment methods under each Amazon account. This authorization will not affect any payment settings of respective Amazon accounts. Account holders can copy the payment method of the other Amazon account to their Amazon account.

If Content Sharing is disabled, the payment methods copied to that Amazon account from another will automatically be removed.

You can link Amazon accounts to create an Amazon Household using the steps below:

1. On the toolbar tap the **Quick Actions** icon, and then tap **All Settings**.
2. Select **Household & Family Library**.
3. Select **Add a New Person**. Then **Add Adult**.
4. Share your Kindle with the person (adult) that you would like to be added to your Kindle Household. Ensure they enter the email address and password of their Amazon account. If the other person does not have an Amazon account, they can create one by visiting the Amazon website.
5. Once the other person enters the email address and password, sharing will be enabled. It's possible to choose whether they would like to share all the purchased content or only selected titles with you.

   Important: The other person will be authorizing you to use any payment methods set up on their Amazon account for Amazon purchases by choosing to enable sharing.

6. The Kindle will prompt the other adult to return the device to you. Then you can proceed by enabling sharing.

Creating a Child Profile for Your Amazon Household

It's possible to have up to four child profiles under your Amazon Household which will enable you to choose and share content with your children.

You can create a child profile by following the steps below:

1. On the toolbar tap the **Quick Actions** icon, and then select **All Settings**.
2. Select **Household & Family Library**.
3. Choose the **Add a New Person** prompt at the bottom of the screen.
   Note: If you already have the maximum number of child profiles in your Kindle Household, adding a new child profile option will be disabled.

4. Tap **Add Child** and enter your parental control password. Enter your child's name, birthday and gender.
5. Choose the content that would like to share to your child's library and tap **Next**.
6. You can review your child's profile and reading settings before tapping **Done**.
   Note: You must be connected to a wireless connection in order to access any profile created using the Amazon website.

Leaving an Amazon Household from Your Kindle E-Reader

To leave an Amazon Household and stop sharing all of your content and payment methods:

1. Tap the **Quick Actions** icon, located on the toolbar, and then **All Settings**.
2. Select **Household & Family Library**.
3. Select the profile that you want to remove from Kindle Household.
4. If prompted, enter the password for the profile.
5. Select **Leave Household**. Confirm by tapping **OK**.

Once you leave Amazon Household, both adults will lose access to the shared content, payment methods and Prime benefits shared by the other adult.

Unlinking Amazon accounts and stop sharing your content and payment methods:

Removing an Adult from Your Amazon Household

If either adult leaves an Amazon Household, they will be unable to join another Household with another person for 180 days.

Follow these instructions to leave a Household and stop sharing your content and privileges:

1. Go to Manage Your Household (https://www.amazon.com/myh/manage) in **Your Account**.
2. Select the adult tab to the left of the page. You can either leave the Household or remove the other adult from the Household:
   - Click **Leave** below your name to remove your account from the Household.
   - Click **Remove** below the other adult's name in order to remove him/her from the Household.

Note: Visit Manage Your Household if you wish to rejoin a Household with the same person.

Setting Up Parental Controls on Kindle E-Reader

You can restrict access to the Kindle Store, the Experimental Web Browser, Cloud and Goodreads with Parental Controls.

Once Parental Controls are enabled, deregistering the Kindle, resetting it, modifying Household & Family Library Settings will be disabled from your device.

You can continue to purchase content through your computer and have it delivered to your device when access to the Kindle Store is locked on your device.

Setting up parental controls:

1. On the toolbar tap the **Quick Actions** icon, and then tap **All Settings**.
2. Tap **Device Options** followed by **Parental Controls**. Then tap **Restrictions**.
3. Selecting **On** will require a password to access to the experimental web browser, Kindle Store, Cloud or Goodreads on your Kindle.
4. Enter your preferred parental controls password. Then tap **OK**.
5. Tap **OK** again to save your settings.

Once you set parental controls, a lock icon will appear at the top of the screen.

Forgot Kindle E-Reader Passcode

You will need to reset your Kindle device in the case of forgetting the on-device passcode.

In you have forgotten the password for your Kindle Paperwhite, you will need to reset your device. Resetting your device will remove the following:

- Personal information, including your lock screen passcode and parental controls
- Amazon account information
- Wi-Fi settings
- Downloaded content

The content that you have purchased from Amazon is automatically saved to the Cloud. Therefore, it can be restored to your device via the **All** tab once you re-register your device to Amazon.

To reset your device
1. Click the password field.
2. Enter **111222777**. Then tap **OK**.

Connect to a wireless network and register your device to use it again.

Resetting Your Password

If you cannot remember your password, you can request a personalized 'password reset' link to be sent to your e-mail address.

When updating the password from a computer unfamiliar to Amazon, you will be asked to confirm your account information before creating the new password.

Requesting a password reset:
1. Go to Forgot Your Password (https://www.amazon.com/gp/css/account/forgot-password/email.html).
2. Follow the on-screen prompts.
3. Follow the directions in the e-mail sent to the e-mail address associated with your account.

Note: If your account was created with a mobile phone number, you will receive instructions via SMS message instead of an e-mail.

Your new password will become active immediately and applies to all Amazon related accounts.

Tip: Choose a strong password. See the section below for details about how to choose a password.

Choosing a Strong Password

It is recommended you periodically change your password to ensure that no one else can gain access to your Amazon account.

Choosing a strong password:
- Create a password that is unique. If you think you may have trouble recalling your password, note it down and store it in a secure location.
- Set a password containing at least 8 characters.
- Previously used passwords will be rejected. Make sure that your password is original.
  Avoid generic passwords that are simple to guess. Your password should not contain your personal information or email address.
    Tip: Add numbers and/or special characters to your password to make it stronger.

Note: Passwords are case sensitive. Ensure that the CAPS LOCK key is not set without your knowledge when creating a password.

About Kindle Books

The Kindle store has many books, textbooks, magazines and newspapers, and audio books available for purchase. Some books may have special features designed to enhance your reading experience. You will also be able to access Kindle-exclusive content on occasion. With the Kindle Unlimited option, you will have unlimited access to thousands of Kindle books.

Types of Kindle Books

Kindle Samples

You can download a free preview of a book before you commit to buying it.

Samples which you download from the Kindle Store are saved to your Cloud account. You can read them on any supported Amazon and Kindle device.

Samples can be sent to a registered device or reading app on your account and then deleted from your content library. Further information can be found at Manage Your Content and Devices (https://www.amazon.com/mycd).

Note: You may need to download the latest software update to ensure smooth operation.

1. Follow the steps to send a sample to your device or reading app:
   - **From your computer**: Head to the Kindle Store (https://www.amazon.com/gp/browse.html?node=133141011). Search for a book that you're interested in. Select **Deliver to:** to access a drop-down menu to select your device or reading app from the product detail page of the book. Finally, tap the **Send sample now** button.
   - **From your device or reading app**: Head to the Kindle Store to search for the book that you're interested in. Select the **Try a Sample** or **Download Sample** button.
2. To delete the sample:
   - **From a supported Amazon device or Kindle reading app**: Press and hold the sample. Choose the option to delete the sample from your device or reading app. You can also delete any samples from the cloud that are on devices linked to your account.
   - You must select the sample(s) that you want to delete and then select **Delete** from Manage Your Content and Devices (https://www.amazon.com/mycd). Select **Yes, delete permanently** from the prompt that appears on your screen.

Audible Audiobooks

Purchase Audible Titles
Audible audiobooks on Amazon are available to purchase with a default 1-Click payment method or existing Audible credits and coupons.

30

Note: Purchases are billed directly by Audible. Audible titles cannot be purchased using an Amazon.com gift card nor can they be transferred to another party.

To purchase an Audible title from Amazon:

1. Go to www.amazon.com/audible.
2. Browse Audible's selection or search for an audiobook that you'd like to purchase.
3. Purchase the audiobook.

   - **If you're not an Audible member:** You will have to select **Start your free trial** or **Buy with 1-Click**. After selecting a free trial, your payment method will be charged after the trial ends, unless you cancel your subscription prior. If you purchase an Audible edition with 1-Click, you will be charged the full price for the audiobook immediately.
   Note: As a previously enrolled in an Audible trial, you will have the option to **buy with membership**. In that case, you just need to select this option and after that you will be charged the current membership fee.

   - **If you're currently an Audible member:** Simply select **Buy with 1 Audible Credit** or **Buy with 1-Click**. If you have no remaining credits on your Audible account, the option to purchase with an Audible credit will be unavailable for you.

After purchasing an Audible title, it can be downloaded anytime to a compatible device.

Link an Existing Audible Account to Your Amazon Account

If you have Audible account you can link it to your Amazon account. You can access your Audible credits or coupons on Amazon, or manage your audiobooks from Manage Your Content and Devices (https://www.amazon.com/mycd).

Important: Occasionally, your existing Audible username will no longer work after linking your Amazon and Audible accounts.

Here are the steps to link your Amazon and Audible accounts:

1. Go to www.audible.com/acc-merge and enter your Audible username and password.
2. Next, enter your Amazon account email address and password.
3. Enter the credit card details you wish to use as the **Default Card** for Audible purchases and membership charges.

Both your Amazon and Audible accounts will be linked after confirming your payment details and billing address. Any audiobooks that you've purchased from Audible will appear in **Manage Your Content and Devices** on Amazon.

Kindle Active Content

You can add software with Kindle active content, such as compatible games to your Kindle e-reader.

Publishers may occasionally release updated more efficient versions of their titles. Previously purchased active content titles can be updated from the Amazon product detail page.

Some steps to update a Kindle active content title:

1. Go to the title's product detail page on Amazon.com.
2. Check to see if an update is available by clicking the **Update Available option**.
3. Select Kindle that you'd like to send the updated version to and click **Go**.

Kindle Scout

With Kindle Scout, you get the opportunity to read excerpts from unpublished manuscripts and vote for your favorites to be published to Kindle. If a book you voted for is published, you will receive a copy of that for free.

Follow the steps below to get started with Kindle Scout:

1. Sign in at kindlescout.amazon.com by entering your Amazon account information.
2. Read excerpts of the available Kindle Scout books and click Nominate Me to request your favorites to be published. You can select up to three books at a time.

The detail page of each book will display how many days remain on the book's campaign. You will receive an email notification if the title you nominated is selected to be published and details on how to receive your free version.

Kindle Serials

Published at regular intervals, Kindle Serials are delivered to your Kindle as they are written by the author.

Kindle Serials contain multiple episodes. When you purchase a Kindle Serial, you will automatically receive all existing episodes. Future episodes will be delivered as they are published at no extra cost. You can also connect with other Kindle Serials readers in the forum to discuss episodes.

Kindle Serials are compatible with all Kindle devices and reading apps. Following the purchase of a Kindle Serial title, it will appear in your content library and will download to your device when it connects to a wireless network. The book will automatically update each time a future episode is released.

Download New Episodes

An e-mail will alert you to the release of a new episode. Some episodes will be available weekly, bi-weekly, or monthly. The details page will indicate the schedule for release.

When the episodes are available they will be automatically delivered to your Kindle. Your device must be connected to a wireless network.

Kindle Singles

Kindle Singles are eBooks of a defined length and a focused theme. They can be accessed from Fire and Kindle devices, Kindle reading apps and on Amazon.

Kindle Singles are lengthier than a typical magazine feature but smaller than the length of most books. Titles are hand-picked and added on a continuing basis.

Kindle Singles offer the same functionality as other Kindle Books and are automatically stored in Manage Your Content and Devices (https://www.amazon.com/mycd) as well.

Kindle Worlds

Kindle Worlds is a Kindle program for publishing. It provides a platform for authors to write stories inspired by featured Worlds including: popular books, shows, movies, comics, music, and games. Authors are given the opportunity to incorporate copyright-protected material into their books and can earn royalties on stories published.

Submit Stories in Kindle Worlds

Authors can publish stories on featured Worlds and earn royalty payments. As an author you can use the Kindle Worlds Self-Service Submission Platform to submit your original works for publication. Follow the below steps:

1. Go to the Self-Service Submission Platform at kindleworlds.amazon.com
2. Select a World in which to write, read the content guidelines and then write your story.
3. Upload and submit your story.

Buy and Download Stories in Kindle Worlds

Kindle Worlds stories are available from the Kindle Words Store (https://www.amazon.com/kindleworlds). World stories can be accessed from all compatible Kindle devices. You can easily search for Kindle World stories by using the search feature or checking the detail pages.

Pottermore Content on Kindle

The Harry Potter series is available for purchase through Pottermore. You can download and read the books on Fire and Kindle devices.

Harry Potter books are available in English (U.S.), Danish, Dutch, French, German, Hungarian, Indonesian, Italian, Japanese, Polish, Portuguese, Spanish and Swedish.

Note: At the time of printing, Polish titles are not compatible with Fire and Kindle devices.

Note: If you are an eligible Amazon Prime member, Harry Potter books are available to borrow for free via the Kindle Owners' Lending Library.

Buy and Download Harry Potter Books from Pottermore

Your book can be transferred to your Kindle library following purchase from the Pottermore (https://www.pottermore.com) website.

34

On the Pottermore site, you can:

1. Purchase Harry Potter books:
- Go to the Kindle Store (https://www.amazon.com/gp/browse.html?node=133141011) and locate your preferred Harry Potter title.
- If the title you are searching for is unavailable through Amazon, you might find it available for purchase through Pottermore. In this instance a **Buy at Pottermore** button will appear on the product detail page on Amazon. Simply click the **Buy at Pottermore** button to open Pottermore.
- Select the Harry Potter book that you want to purchase and click **Buy now** from Pottermore. Continue shopping by clicking **Continue Shopping**.
- When you are ready to finalize your purchases, click **Checkout** to place your order.
- You will receive a confirmation e-mail from Pottermore when your order has been placed.
2. Steps that help you to download Harry Potter books:

   - **Download Your Books** from the Pottermore confirmation page.
   - Select **Transfer to Your Amazon Library**.
   - Enter your Amazon account information and click **Sign in using our secure server**.
   - Click the link to **Go to Amazon** on the confirmation message.
   - Click the **Actions** button next to your book and then tap **Deliver** to wirelessly send your Pottermore book to your registered device or reading app.

Your Harry Potter book(s) will now be available for all the Fire & Kindle devices and Kindle reading apps registered to your Amazon account.

Note: You will need to individually download each title when purchasing multiple Harry Potter books.

Content Subscriptions

About Kindle Unlimited

Using the Kindle Unlimited subscription allows you to access a large selection of titles from the Kindle Store.

You have access to over one million titles in the Kindle Store with a Kindle Unlimited subscription including books, audiobooks and magazines. Your Amazon account can be used to browse and borrow up to ten titles and access them from any Amazon device or Kindle reading app, even while travelling. An advantage to using Kindle Unlimited is there are no applicable due dates. Cataloged titles may change without notice.

Kindle Unlimited subscription offers a free 30-day trial. At the end of the free trial period, your account is automatically upgraded to a monthly paid subscription.

Head to Manage or Cancel Your Kindle Unlimited Membership (https://www.amazon.com/gp/help/customer/display.html?nodeId=201588170) to manage or cancel your subscription.

You can pay in your subscription in advance or give a subscription to another as a gift.

If you have received a Kindle Unlimited subscription as a gift or as part of a bundle, you will be prompted to upgrade to a paid plan at the end of your prepaid subscription.

You must have an Amazon account with a current, valid credit card to use Kindle Unlimited and enable 1-Click. Follow the below steps to set up the 1-Click payment method:

1. Go to Manage Your Content and Devices (https://www.amazon.com/mycd).
2. Select the **Settings** tab
3. Select the **Edit Payment Method** tab located below **Digital Payment Settings**.

Titles in the Kindle Unlimited catalog are subject change.

Important: Kindle Unlimited is not associated with Prime Reading which is a content borrowing service exclusively for Amazon Prime Members.

Download a Kindle Unlimited Title
Here is process involved in borrowing a Kindle Unlimited title from your device:

1. Open the **Kindle Store**.
2. Access the Kindle Unlimited catalog:
   - Kindle e-readers: Select **All Categories** and then select **Kindle Unlimited**.
   - Fire tablets: Select **Kindle Unlimited**.
   - Kindle reading apps: Select **Kindle Unlimited**.
3. Select **Read for Free** after choosing a title. The Kindle Unlimited logo will be visible on eligible titles.

To borrow Kindle Unlimited titles from the Amazon website:

1. Go to the Kindle Unlimited browse (https://www.amazon.com/b?node=9069934011) page or find a title by searching for the Kindle Unlimited logo.
2. Select **Read for Free** from the product detail page of the Kindle Unlimited title.

Return a Kindle Unlimited Title

There are no due dates if you borrow titles from the Kindle Unlimited catalog.

Using your supported Amazon device or the web browser on your computer or mobile device it is easy to return Kindle Unlimited content at any time.

Returning content from your supported Amazon device:

1. Open the **Kindle Store**.
2. Select **Kindle Unlimited** on Kindle e-readers.
3. Select **View My Kindle Unlimited Library** and then **Return** next to the title.

Here are the steps to return content from your web browser:

1. Go to Manage Your Content and Devices (https://www.amazon.com/mycd).
2. Using the drop-down menu from the **Your Content** tab to filter by **Kindle Unlimited**.
3. Select the **Actions** button next to the title you want to return and then tap **Return this title**.

Kindle Unlimited Audiobooks

Kindle Unlimited books includes access to a free audiobook companion guide.

You can listen to Kindle Unlimited audiobooks on most Kindle Devices, free Kindle reading apps and the Audible app.

Kindle unlimited titles that include the free Whispersync for Voice audiobook will upgrade display a "with narration" icon. Titles that include 'with narration' are free.

You can also easily browse all audiobooks that are free with Kindle Unlimited on the Amazon website.

Some Kindle Unlimited books have synced audiobooks, as well as Whispersync for Voice upgrades, which may include an extra fee.

You can find all Whispersync voice upgrades by selecting **Whispersync for Voice** under **Refine by** on the left side of the Kindle Unlimited browse (https://www.amazon.com/b/ref=s9_al_bw_brwse?_encoding=UTF8&node=906 9934011).

Kindle Magazines and Newspapers

The Kindle store on Kindle and Fire devices supports Kindle reading apps and the Amazon website and facilitates the easy subscription of magazines and newspapers.

Subscriptions are based on a minimum 14-day free trial period, which you can elect to cancel at any time during your trial period without charge. If you do not cancel your subscription, your default 1-Click payment method will be debited. You can to cancel your paid subscription at any time. Subscriptions require a credit card to purchase.

Device availability and frequency of delivery information is provided on the product details page of magazines and newspapers. You require a wireless connection to automatically receive subscription content.

Manage Your Subscription Settings

Magazine and newspaper subscriptions are offered on a monthly or annual basis. If you fail to cancel your annual subscription it will automatically renew at the end of the subscribed period. Monthly subscriptions renew at the end of each month unless otherwise cancelled.

Download Past Issues from the Cloud

Back issues of magazines and newspapers are stored on the cloud and can be easily downloaded – even once your subscription has ended. To access a back issue from a computer, follow the steps below:

1. Go to **MYCD** and select your subscription type (magazine/newspaper,) from the dropdown menu.
2. Tap the **Actions** button next to the subscription name. Then select either **Deliver past issue to my...** to deliver an issue wirelessly or **Download and transfer past issue via USB** to transfer via USB.
3. Select the issue you want and then choose the device to which you want the issue delivered.
4. Tap **Deliver**.

Older issues of newspapers and magazines will be removed automatically at the time of downloading the new issues, unless you choose to save them. There are two steps to store issues on your device:

1. Find the issue that you'd like to keep on your device from the Home screen.
2. Select the **Keep This Issue** option, press and hold.

Kindle Subscription Formats and Special Content

The Kindle Store has a variety of magazine and newspaper formats, such as video, audio, slideshows and more.

You can select page view on Fire tablets, Kindle for iPad, iPhone and iPod touch and Kindle for Android to view a replica of the printed edition of the magazine. You can zoom in on the text for more accessible reading.

Tip: Selected magazine apps are available in the **Newsstand,** on Fire (except Kindle Fire 1st Generation).

The New York Times, The New Yorker and The Wall Street Journal subscribers can gain access to additional features and view the publisher's online archive. These links that provide more information about special access to these publications:

- The New York Times Access (https://www.nytimes.com/content/help/account/purchases/kindle/kindle-subscribers.html)
- The New Yorker Access (https://subscriptions.newyorker.com/pubs/N3/NYR/digital_auth-noacct-nyr.jsp?cds_page_id=112377)
- The Wall Street Journal Kindle Digital Plus (https://iwap.wsj.com/kindlexp/FAQ.do)

Pre-Order, Deals, and Offers

Kindle Countdown Deals

Kindle Countdown Deals provide limited-time promotional discounts on eBooks published exclusively for Kindle.

A "Countdown Clock" on the product detail page will indicate the remaining time to purchase a title at the promotional price. Once the promotion ends, the book is back to full price again.

You can find a list of active Kindle Countdown Deals at Kindle Countdown Deals (http://www.amazon.com/kindlecountdowndeals).

The "Countdown Clock" will appear near the pricing information on your Kindle eReader.

Amazon First Reads

Amazon First Reads allows members to download a Kindle book from our editors' picks each month before the official publication date, for $1.99—Prime members can receive it for free. General customers can also shop editors' picks in hardcover at exclusive prices. New titles are announced on the 1st of each month.

If you have an Amazon Prime membership then you can do the following:

- Download the Amazon First Reads title of your choice for free. You will be automatically eligible for the Amazon First Reads program with Amazon Prime (https://www.amazon.com/prime) (including regular, discounted, free trial, or invitee Amazon Prime memberships). Download one free title per month, up to one month before its official release date.

- You can shop all six hardcover edition Amazon First Reads titles at exclusive prices.

You can join Amazon First Reads even if you do not have an Amazon Prime membership, by subscribing to the Amazon First Reads email newsletter. More about this offer follows:

- Receive information about new Amazon First Reads titles.
- Each month, you can purchase a Kindle title of your choice one month prior to their release date, for $1.99.
- Shop for all six Amazon First Reads titles in hardcover edition at exclusive prices.

Amazon First Reads Kindle downloads are limited to one per month and do not rollover from previous months. At the standard Kindle Pre-Order Purchase Price, you can pre-order any additional selections.

Amazon First Reads titles cannot be gifted.

Kindle Unlimited subscribers can borrow Amazon First Reads books at no cost following their release (one month after they are available with the Amazon First Reads program).

Locate Amazon First Reads on Your Device
- Tap **Shop in Kindle Store** and then select **Amazon First Reads**.

Subscribe to the Amazon First Reads Newsletter
Here are the steps to subscribe to the Amazon First Reads monthly newsletter:

1. Go to Amazon First Reads (https://www.amazon.com/firstreads).
2. Click **Sign up for the monthly e-mail**.

Unsubscribe from the Amazon First Reads Newsletter
To unsubscribe from the Amazon First Reads monthly newsletter:

1. Go to Your Account (https://www.amazon.com/your-account) and then click **Email** under the **Email alerts, messages, and ads** section.
2. Click **Unsubscribe** next to Amazon First Reads.
   Note: Unsubscribing from the newsletter does not affect your eligibility to download one free book each month as an Amazon Prime member.

Kindle MatchBook

There are thousands of qualifying books and past or present print edition purchase now lets you buy the Kindle edition for $2.99 or less. (Textbooks available for $9.99 or less.)

Kindle MatchBook allows customers who have previously purchased a physical book from Amazon.com to purchase the Kindle version for $2.99 or less. (Textbooks available for $9.99 or less.) This only applies to eligible physical books purchased in new condition from Amazon.com and is not available for third-party sellers. Customers who purchase multiple copies of a physical book are limited to one Kindle copy.

Important: Only new books are eligible for the Kindle MatchBook program. Third-party sellers are excluded from this offer. Books purchased from physical Amazon Books stores ineligible.

Eligible Kindle MatchBook titles will display the Kindle MatchBook logo on the product details page as well as at Kindle MatchBook (https://www.amazon.com/kindlematchbook). From the Kindle Store (https://www.amazon.com/b/?&node=1286228011), you can buy the Kindle edition for Kindle MatchBook on the Amazon website, Fire and Kindle devices, or anywhere you currently buy Kindle books.

Kindle MatchBooks titles can be read on your Fire or Kindle device or on your computer, tablet or phone with a Kindle Reading App (https://www.amazon.com/gp/feature.html/?docId=1000493771).

Note: You must be signed into the same account the physical book was purchased from, for the MatchBook price to be available.

Read While Your Book Ships

After purchasing a new physical book from Amazon, you can read a sample on your e-readers and Kindle reading apps, or on your browser.

Here are the steps to read your sample:

- Select **Start Reading** on the **Thank You** page following your purchase of a new physical book from Amazon.
  - **Note:** When you purchase a physical book from your desktop browser or mobile browser on Android and iOS devices, the **Start Reading** option will appear to you.

- Select **Start Reading**, the sample will be available in the Cloud on e-readers and Kindle reading apps which is registered to your account. A sample may also open in the browser of your device.

If you forget to download your sample immediately after purchasing a physical book, you can download again the sample from the Kindle book detail page on Amazon.

Pre-Order a Kindle Book

You can order your selected Kindle books before their release date from the Kindle Store.

A **Pre-Order** button on the Kindle book detail page will be indicate that it is a pre-order item.

After completing your pre-order for a Kindle book, your 1-Click payment method will be charged for the content.

To pre-order a Kindle book:

1. Open the detail page of the Kindle book that you'd like to pre-order.
2. Select **Pre-order: Add to Cart** or **Pre-order with 1-Click**.

You will receive an e-mail notification to confirm pre-order. You will be notified again by e-mail once the Kindle book is released and available in your Kindle library.

To cancel your pre-order before the release date open Your Digital Orders (https://www.amazon.com/digitalorders), find the pre-order and then select **Cancel Items**.

Note: At the time of releasing the book and placing your order, the price you pay will be the lowest price offered by Amazon.com.

Buy, Download & Sync

Buy & Download Kindle Content from Kindle E-Reader

You can buy content on the Kindle Store and download that content to your device only when you are connected to a wireless network.

Purchased content is automatically downloaded to allow immediate reading. Content is also stored in the Cloud, enabling you to download it to other compatible registered devices or Kindle reading apps.

Tip: Go to Parental Control to learn about preventing accidental purchases.

To purchase Kindle content from your device:

1. Connect your Kindle to a wireless network.
    Tip: You can download content faster when you're connected to a Wi-Fi network, although it's still possible to buy and download content when you are connected to a 3G network.

2. Tap the **Store** store icon.
3. Browse the Kindle store for content or search for a specific title.
4. Tap **Buy** to purchase a title. In order to subscribe to a newspaper or a magazine, tap **Subscribe now**.
    Tip: You can download the beginning of a book by tapping **Try a Sample** for free.

5. Select the **Home** icon. Click **Downloaded** to open and view your content.

Note: The Kindle content will be automatically added to the **All** tab on your Kindle. Once a download is complete, your content will appear on the **Downloaded** tab. Larger files may take longer to download.

Sync and Download Content on Your Kindle

Receive updated content to your Kindle by syncing the device through Manage Your Content and Devices (https://www.amazon.com/mycd). You can

44

also synchronize content progress across devices as well as download any available software updates.

Content purchased through the Kindle Store will be saved to your content library in the Cloud. Ensure your Kindle device is connected to a wireless network in order to download content or software updates.

Follow the steps below to receive Kindle content:

1. Select the **Quick Actions** icon on the Kindle Home screen.
2. Click **Sync My Kindle**.

All the titles sent to your Kindle as well as saved bookmarks and annotations should start downloading to your Kindle device.

The most recent page read across all devices and Kindle reading apps registered to your Amazon account will sync by default.

You can manually sync to the most recent page read:

1. While reading, tap the **Quick Actions** icon.
2. Click **Sync My Kindle**.

You can receive the latest available software version:

1. Ensure your Kindle is charging during the update.
2. Connect your device to Wi-Fi network. Downloading will automatically begin, even if your Kindle device is in Sleep Mode.
3. Ensure your Kindle device is connected to the Wi-Fi network and a power source until the update is complete.

Note: Your Kindle may restart multiple times during a software update.

Sync Across Fire & Kindle Devices and Apps

Whispersync can synchronize your content across supported devices and apps.

Whispersync backs up your data and furthest read location to the Cloud on supported devices and apps, making it easy to access your content and pick up where you left off on another supported app or device registered to the same account.

The following content categories are supported by Whispersync:

- Books from the Kindle Store
  - Personal documents that are converted to Kindle format
  - Newspapers and magazines from the Kindle Store
  - Audiobooks from Audible.com
  - Prime Video
  - Apps and games from Amazon Appstore

Sync Your Books & Personal Documents Automatically

Whispersync for Books is allows you to stop reading on one device and pick up where you left off on another. Both devices have to be registered to the same account. Whispersync for Books is enabled as a default function.

Whispersync will allow you to view bookmarks, highlights and notes that were created on devices registered to the same amazon account. It will automatically sync your last page read and annotations for personal documents that are converted to kindle format.

To enable or disable Whispersync:

1. Go to Manage Your Content and Devices (https://www.amazon.com/mycd).
2. Select the **Settings** tab.
3. Under **Device Synchronization (Whispersync Settings)**, set **Whispersync Device Synchronization** to **ON** or **OFF**.

To avoid syncing errors:

- Ensure your device is connected to a wireless network for automatic syncing across your Fire & Kindle devices and Kindle reading apps. To disable the wireless connection, you have to turn it off instead using sleeping mode.
- When your reading is complete, return to the **Home** screen on your device.
- Regularly back up your annotations to view your bookmarks, highlights and notes on other devices.

Back Up Your Bookmarks, Notes & Highlights

Automatically back up your bookmarks, notes, and highlights to your Kindle Library in the Cloud. You can then view them on Fire tablets, Kindle e-readers and Kindle reading apps that are registered to the same Amazon account. Your notes and highlights are included in Popular Highlights.

Check with your Kindle e-readers and Kindle reading apps to see if Annotations Backup is enabled.

Here are the steps to back up your bookmarks, notes, and highlights on your Kindle e-reader or Kindle reading app:

1. Ensure that Whispersync is enabled.
2. Go to the **Home** screen to select the **Menu** button or icon and then select **Settings** from your Kindle e-reader or Kindle reading app.
3. Ensure that **Annotations Backup** is ON.

Transfer Kindle Books to Your Kindle via USB

If you are unable to connect to a Wi-Fi network, you can transfer Kindle books, magazines and newspapers from a computer via USB.

Content that has been purchased from the Kindle Store is stored in the Cloud. It is available for transfer from Manage Your Content and Devices (https://www.amazon.com/mycd).

Follow these steps to transfer content from a computer to your Kindle:

1. Go to Manage Your Content and Devices (https://www.amazon.com/mycd). Select the content that you would like to transfer to your Kindle.
2. Select the **Actions** button next to the title. Click **Download & Transfer via USB**.
3. Select your Kindle from the drop down menu and then click **Download**.
   Important: Remember the location of folder that you download your content file to as you will need to transfer the content to your Kindle from this folder.

4. Using the USB cable, connect your Kindle to your computer. Your Kindle device will appear in the same location on your computer as a normal external USB drive will appear.
   o **Windows**: Your Kindle will appear in the **Computer** or **My Computer** folder.
   o **Mac**: Your Kindle will appear on the desktop.

5. Open the **Kindle** folder. Then open the **documents** folder.

6. Click the downloaded file on your computer and drag and drop the compatible file into the **Documents** folder within the **Kindle** folder.

7. Safely eject your Kindle from your computer.

8. On touch-screen devices, you can view the downloaded content on the **Downloaded** tab.

Transfer Documents to Your Kindle via USB

Transfer compatible documents from your computer to your Kindle e-reader.

Follow these steps to transfer a document to your device:

- Connect your Kindle device to your computer via the USB cable. Your Kindle device will appear in the same location on your computer as a normal external USB drive will appear.
    - **Windows**: Your device will appear in the **Computer** or **My Computer** folder.
    - **Mac**: Your device will appear on the desktop.
- Open the **Documents** or **Internal Documents** folder in the device folder. **Note:** The folder names will vary depending on your device type.

- Click the document file on your computer and then drag and drop the file into the desired device folder.
- Once the file has completed transferring, safely disconnect your Kindle device from your computer.

The transferred document/s will appear on the Home screen of your Kindle e-reader.

Read on Your Kindle Paperwhite

Reading Basics

Understanding Kindle Display Technology

Your Kindle is outfitted with a high-resolution display technology called electronic paper. This technology allows you to read clearly even if bright areas due to the reflective nature of the display screen. You might witness the screen flash occasionally as the e-reader page display refreshes. Your Kindle display features fast and smooth page turns while minimizing the number of page refreshes. To refresh at every page turn, tap the Quick Actions icon on the toolbar and then tap All Settings. Select Reading Options and adjust the Page Refresh setting. For manga, comics and picture books, tap the Menu icon while reading and then tap Page Refresh On/Off setting.

View Your Reading Progress

View the pages read or the percentage of the book remaining while reading.

Use your Kindle to calculate your reading speed and estimate how much time it will take to finish a chapter or a book using the Time To Read feature. Reading speed is only stored on your Kindle and is not stored on Amazon servers.

Follow the steps below to use Time to Read:

1. Tap the top of the screen to bring up the reading toolbar while reading.
2. Click the **Display Settings** (Aa) icon. Then tap the **Reading Progress** tab.
3. Select your preferred tracking option while will be displayed at the bottom of your screen from the options below:
    - **Location in book**
    - **Page in book** (if available)
    - **Time left in chapter**
    - **Time left in book**
    - **None**

Note: For Kindle books, real page numbers are not available.

Go to Other Locations in a Book

You can instantly navigate to the **Beginning** or **End** of the book while reading by tapping the **Go To** icon in the reading toolbar. You also move to a specific **Chapter**, **Page**, or **Location** if available.

Read complete footnotes without changing the page or drifting away from where you are by simply tapping a footnote. Tap **Go to Footnotes** to see all the footnotes.

Using the Page Flip function, you can skim pages and jump back and forth without losing track of where you are.

Follow these steps to use Page Flip for supported titles:

1. Access the reading toolbar by tapping the top of the screen. Clicking the bottom of the screen will launch a preview window and a progress bar.
2. Use the preview window to see other locations in the book with these steps:
    *   Swipe within the Preview Window or tap the left or right arrows in the window.
    *   Use the in-progress bar at the bottom of the screen by holding and dragging it left or right.
3. Go to a specific location in a book by tapping a page in the Preview Window. Return to the current page in the book by tapping **X** in the top-right corner.

Press and hold the screen to launch the on-screen slide bar when reading Manga or Comics. Slide the bar to the right or to the left to navigate through pages.

Change Fonts Line Spacing or Margins

Change fonts, font size, line spacing or margins of the page display to make reading easier.

Note: You can't modify the text size of menus and other screens, nor can you change the text appearance of PDF files.

1. Tap the top of the screen to launch the reading toolbar and then tap **Aa**.
2. Select the text size and font from the **Font** tab.
    *   Font sizes range from 8-point size to 36-point size.
    *   Select the desired boldness level for certain fonts.
    *   Read the book in the Publisher Font when available.
    *   A Dyslexic Font option is available for many books including Kindle Samples.
3. Set the line spacing and margins from the **Page** tab:
    *   **Spacing** - Choose the amount of space above and below each line.
    *   **Margins** – Choose the amount of space on the left and right sides of each page.
    *   **Orientation** – You can view your content either vertically or horizontally.
    *   **Alignment** - Select your preferred text alignment.
4. Tap the **X** in the top-right corner to return to reading.

Comics

Use a pinching motion to zoom in and out when reading comic books. Navigate panels by swiping your finger across the screen or tapping the edges of the screen. Enter Kindle Panel View by double tapping the screen when reading a comic book. Kindle Panel View must be enabled first for Manga books.

Tap the Menu item and then click the Virtual Panel setting to **On** while reading a Manga book. You can now enter Kindle Panel View by double tapping the screen. Select the Menu item and tap on Page Refresh On/Off setting to access page refresh settings. Advanced page turn control is now available for thousands of books for an improved manga experience. Quickly turn pages by pressing and holding.. Adjust the speed and direction by dragging left and right. Each day, more books that support these improvements are being added.

Kindle organizes your library by automatically grouping comics content by series. The cover of each book you most recently interacted with will represent the series in your library. An icon in the lower left corner will display the number of books from that series that you own or have downloaded.

Tap on the cover image to view a list of the books and access it as a series grouping. Series grouping provides options for sorting such as series reading order (ascending/descending) and release date (ascending/descending).

Disable this feature by tapping the Quick Actions icon on the tool bar, and then All Settings. Tap Device Options on the Settings page and then Advanced Options and select Group Comics by Series.

Any incorrectly grouped items can be reported by long pressing on the cover of the book and tapping Submit Series Feedback to let Kindle know.

Children's Books

A Text Pop-Up feature is available for some Kindle children's books, for reading text over images. Swipe your finger across the screen or tap the sides to navigate between Text Pop-Up sections.

Exit Text Pop-Up and return to normal reading by double tapping the screen.

Images

To increase the size of an image press and hold your finger on it to launch a magnifying glass. Select from a series of options including Highlight, Note, Share and Search. View more options such as Report Content Error by tapping the Menu icon on the options bar. Re-tap the image return the image to its normal size.

Zoom in further on some Kindle books by placing two fingers on the screen and spreading them apart. Reverse this action to zoom out. While using the zoom in function, navigate the image by dragging your finger to the area of interest. Tap **X** in the top right corner of the image to return back to reading.

Reading Enhancements

To learn more about the book you are reading, use the dictionary to expand your vocabulary, view word hints and translate text with your Kindle.

Use Smart Lookup to Learn More about a Book

Access definitions, characters, settings and more using the Smart Lookup feature on your Kindle without losing track of where you were.

Tapping a word or a phrase and then releasing while reading will launch **Smart Lookup** cards. Smart Lookup identifies the word or phrase you are looking up and adjusts accordingly. Switch between **Smart Lookup** cards by swiping left or right or by tapping another tab to switch cards.

- **Dictionary**: Instantly the definition of a word. If you want to select another dictionary that is installed on your device, tap the name of your dictionary and then click select. You can view the full definition by scrolling within the Dictionary card.

- **X-Ray**: Learn more about a character, term or a concept by tapping **Open X-Ray** to display relevant passages. Filter by **Notable Clips** or **All Mentions**. The location where the character or term is mentioned will be indicated by a series of dots in the timeline. Tap the corresponding dot to go to that location. You can go to a passage by tapping a passage. Click the **Back** < button to return to the X-Ray dialog box or tap the **X** to resume reading.

  Note: For some Kindle books, the **X-Ray** option may be disabled.

- **Wikipedia**: Scroll to the Wikipedia card to view a full description. Tap **Open Wikipedia** to see more information about a concept or word. Your device must be connected to a wireless network in order to use Wikipedia. Return to your book by tapping outside the Smart Lookup window.

- **Translation**: Select a word and tap the **To** drop-down arrow to translate the selected word into Chinese, Danish, Dutch, English, Finnish, French,

German and more. Note: translations are provided by Bing Translator and may not be entirely accurate.

Expand Your Vocabulary

Words you searched in the dictionary are added to the Vocabulary Builder on your Kindle device. Use the flashcards to learn definitions and how to use those words with the Vocabulary Builder.

Note: Only content purchased from the Kindle store or sent through Kindle applications are supported by Vocabulary Builder. Personal documents transferred to your Kindle device via the USB are not supported by the Vocabulary Builder.

Follow the instructions below to use Vocabulary Builder:

1. Tap the **Menu** ⋮ icon on the **Home** menu. Tap **Vocabulary Builder**.
2. Tap to filter the list of words:
   - **Words** tab – Filters all words you have searched in the dictionary.
   - **Books** tab – Filters words you searched in a specific book.
   - **Learning** – Filters available flashcard words.
   - **Mastered** – Filters words you mark as mastered and are no longer included in the flashcards.
3. In order to view the **Dictionary** definition and **Usage**, tap a word from the list. Return to the list by tapping outside the window. Remove a word from the Vocabulary Builder by tapping **Delete**.

Follow these steps to use flashcards:

Tap **Flashcards** and flip through the flashcards by swiping across the screen.

1. Transfer a word from the **Learning** list to the **Mastered** list by tapping **Mark as Mastered**.
2. Return to the full list of words by tapping **Exit Flashcards**.

Turn off Vocabulary Builder by tapping the **Menu** icon and tapping **Settings.** Tap **Reading Options** and then **Language Learning**. Select switch off **Vocabulary Builder**. While the Vocabulary Builder is turned off, words will not be added to it.

See Hints for Difficult Words with Word Wise

Simple explanations and synonyms are displayed above difficult words with Word Wise to make reading easier. It is a useful tool when reading more challenging content.

Note: Word Wise is only available for books written in English and is not available on all books. Check its availability on the product detail pages.

Tap a word to display the dictionary definition of a word or rate the helpfulness of a Word Wise.

Adjust the difficulty of the words showing hints by tapping Word Wise in the lower right corner of the screen while reading. You can drag the slider between 'Fewer Hints' and 'More Hints' as you wish. It's also possible to select Show or Hide hints from this screen.

Follow these steps to turn Word Wise on or off:

1. Tap the **Quick Actions** icon, and then tap **All Settings**.
2. Select **Reading Options** and then **Language Learning**.
3. Tap **On** or **Off** next to **Word Wise**.

Translate Text Using Instant Translations

Translate selected text into a different language while reading by using Instant Translations.

You must be connected to a wireless network to use Instant Translations.
1. Press and drag to highlight the text that you want to translate while reading.
2. Swipe left to the Translation card in the pop-up menu if the **Smart Lookup** window appears. If not, tap **More** (three vertical dots) and then select **Translation**. Select the language to translate the highlighted information.

Bookmarks Highlights & Notes on Kindle E-Reader

Organize bookmarks by adding or removing bookmarks, highlights as well as notes at any location in a Kindle book or personal document on your Kindle device.

Manage Bookmarks

- **Add a bookmark**: To add a bookmark while reading, tap the top-right corner of the screen to show the **Bookmark** icon. Then tap + in the dialog box that opens. Once a page has been bookmarked, the **Bookmark** icon turns black.

- **View your bookmarks**: View your bookmarks by tapping the top-right corner of the screen to see bookmarks. You can also tap the top of the screen to show the Reading Toolbar and tap the **Bookmarks** icon. Tapping a bookmark will launch a preview of the location in the book. You can navigate to that location by tapping the preview window. You can return to where you left off by tapping outside of the preview window.

- **Remove a bookmark**: Remove a bookmark by tapping the top-right corner of the screen and selecting a bookmark from the list that appears and tapping **X** to remove the selected bookmark.

Manage Highlights

- **Add a highlight**: Selected text will be automatically highlighted when you select more than five words. When highlighting across multiple pages, press and drag to the bottom right corner of your screen and the page will turn. The first section of the next page will be automatically highlighted for your convenience.

- **View your highlights**: View highlights by tapping the top of the screen and tapping the ⋮ icon in the Reading Toolbar. Tap **Notes**. Go to the location of a highlight by tapping it.

- **Remove a highlight**: Remove a highlight by tapping is and then tapping **Delete**.

- **Share a highlight**: To Share a highlight, bring up the Reading Toolbar by tapping the top of the screen. Then tap the **Menu** ⋮ icon and tap **Notes**. Tapping **Share** will enable you to share highlights via Goodreads, Facebook or Twitter.

Manage Notes

- **Add** a note:

1. Highlight the text by pressing and holding or dragging a word. Tap **Add Note** and then type your content.
2. Create a note by tapping **Save**.

- **View, Remove, or Edit a note**:
  1. Access the Reading Toolbar by tapping the top of the screen. Then tap the **Menu** ⋮ icon, and **Notes**.

     Tip: You can also access the **Notes** tab by first tapping **Go To** in the reading toolbar.

  2. Tapping a note will navigate you to that location in the book. You can modify or delete a note by tapping **Edit**.

Popular Highlights

Popular highlights of Kindle users and passages with the most highlights are combined and displayed by Amazon.

- **To turn on Popular Highlights:**
  1. Bring up the Reading Toolbar by tapping the top of the screen.
  2. On the toolbar tap the **Quick Actions** ⬡ icon, and then tap **All Settings**.
  3. Tap **Reading Options**. Then tap **Highlights & About This Book**.
  4. Tap **On** next to **Popular Highlights**.

     A selection of highlights that Kindle users have frequently selected will start to appear when you return to reading.

- **To view a list of Popular Highlights:**
  1. Access the Reading Toolbar by tapping the top of your screen.
  2. Tap the **Menu** icon. Then tap **Notes**.

     Tip: You can also tap **Notes** tab by tapping **Go To** in the reading toolbar.

  3. View popular highlights by tapping the **Popular** tab.

Removing items from your Kindle

Free space on your Kindle device by manually removing individual items, items by content type or by archiving them.

Remove individual items by tapping the **Menu** icon on the item's cover when in grid view or on the right side of the screen when in list view. Tap Remove from Device. You can also launch this option by pressing and holding a collection's name or cover.

To change the appearance from grid to list view, simply tap All Items or the currently selected filter and then select List or Grid View.

Remove options change depending on the type of content you are trying to remove. Your content will be safely stored in the Cloud and you can re-download later if required. Note: your personal documents will only be saved in the Cloud if they were emailed to your Kindle and have enabled Personal Document Archiving.

When removing files that were transferred to your Kindle via the USB, they will be permanently deleted from the Kindle device as they are not stored in the Cloud.

You can manually select items by content type or quickly archive items by tapping the Quick Actions icon on the toolbar. Then tap All Settings. On the Settings page, tap Device Options, followed by Advanced Options and then Storage Management.

Manual Removal:

Select items that you want removed based on their content type such as Books, Audiobooks, Periodicals, Docs, Samples and Others.

You will still be able to access the items downloaded from the cloud by tapping **All** on your library. Any items that were manually transferred via the USB cable will be permanently deleted.

Quick Archive:

Quickly free up storage space on your device with the Quick Archive feature by removing items that were downloaded but have not been recently opened.

Access the items downloaded from the cloud by tapping **All** on your library. Any items that were manually transferred via the USB cable will be permanently deleted.

Playing Audible books

You can browse, purchase and listen to Audible books with your Kindle. Purchase audio content directly from your device by going to the Audible Store or by purchasing the Audiobook and Kindle book versions as a bundle from the Kindle Store.

Tap the top your screen to access the toolbar and then tap the Store icon to access the Kindle and Audible Stores. If you are not already an Audible member, you can sign up for membership via the Audible storefront or from the detail page of any Audible book.

Note: Audible-enabled devices are not available in all countries.

Pairing a Bluetooth audio device

Listen to Audible books on your Kindle by paring with a Bluetooth audio device such as headphones or speakers. A Bluetooth audio device can be paired in two methods:

Pairing a Bluetooth Device When Opening an Audiobook

1. From the **Home** screen, tap **My Library** and then tap **Downloaded**.
2. Select the audiobook that you want to listen to by tapping it. You will be prompted to pair with a Bluetooth device if you already have not done so once the **Play** button is pressed.
3. Ensure that your Bluetooth audio device is in pairing mode.
4. Select the Bluetooth device that you want to use by tapping it.
5. The audiobook will play once the Bluetooth audio device is paired.

Pairing a Bluetooth device via Settings

1. Set Bluetooth audio device to pairing mode.
2. Locate and tap **My Library** in the top left of your **Home** screen. Then tap the **Quick Actions** icon on the toolbar and proceed by tapping **All Settings**. Tap Wi-Fi & Bluetooth and then Bluetooth devices on the settings page.
3. Open the downloaded audiobook. Tap No Bluetooth Connected in order to launch the Bluetooth dialog.

Follow the troubleshooting steps below If you are having trouble pairing your device:

- Ensure that your device is turned on and in pairing mode.
- Switch the device off and on again.
- Refresh devices by tapping the Rescan button.
- Dismiss and re-open the Kindle Bluetooth dialog.
- Switch the Bluetooth setting off and on.

Using the Audible Player

Navigate to a section of an audiobook by using the slider at the top of the Audible Player. You can view the time that is left in a particular chapter above the slider. The current chapter name is displayed below the slider.

Rewind: Use this button to rewind thirty seconds.

Play/Pause button: Use this button to **Play** and **Pause** an audiobook directly from your Kindle by tapping it. If supported, it's also possible to control playback from your Bluetooth device.

Fast Forward button: Fast forward in thirty second intervals using this button.

Chapters: Select and listen to any chapter in an audiobook by tapping the chapter. Once a chapter is selected, playback will start from the beginning of the new chapter. This dialog also displays the duration of each chapter.

Volume button: Control the volume on your Kindle using this button. You can also control the volume from your Bluetooth device. Tap in order to increase volume and tap to decrease the volume.

Bluetooth Connected: The Audible Player will display the name of devices connected via Bluetooth. Tapping here also allows you to connect a previously paired Bluetooth device or a new Bluetooth device.

Switch to e-book: This option appears if both the audiobook and Kindle book have been purchased. You can select to switch between reading the book and listening to the book using this option.

Audiobook bookmarks

Tapping the Add Bookmark button for audiobooks located at the bottom of the Audible Player will add a bookmark to the current location in your audiobook. Tap the Add Note button to associate a note with an audiobook bookmark. Tap the Menu icon and select Bookmarks and Notes to view all of the bookmarks and notes for your audiobook.

Tips:

• After selecting a bookmark, it will automatically start playback from that location.

• Edit an existing bookmark by tapping the Menu icon associated with the bookmark and selecting Edit Bookmark.

• If you want to delete an existing bookmark, tap the Menu icon associated with the bookmark and select Delete Bookmark.

Downloading Audible books

Audiobooks can be downloaded directly from the Audible Player. If you own both the audiobook and the Kindle book, but do not have the audiobook on your device, make sure you are connected to Wi-Fi. While reading the Kindle book version, your audiobook will be available to played as soon as the download reaches the location you are currently reading. If you have not started reading or listening to the book, your audiobook will be ready to be played once the download reaches 5%.

You can also download an audiobook using the menu icon. Tap My Library at the top left of your **Home** screen. If you are in grid view, tap the **Menu** icon or if you are in list view, tap the **Menu** icon to the right of the item. Select Download Audible book.

You can download an audiobook without a companion Kindle book by tapping My Library in the top left of your **Home** screen. Start the download by tapping the book cover. You can start listening to the audiobook once the download reaches 5%.

You can cancel a download by tapping My Library in the top left of your **Home** screen. First tap the **Menu** icon and then select Cancel Download. It's also possible to cancel the download from the Audible Player by tapping the Cancel icon found on the cover of the book.

Audiobook Library Management

If you own both the audiobook and the companion of Kindle book; they will appear as one item in your library and a pair of headphones will display to the right of the book name when in List view or shown on the top right of the cover when in Grid view. Please remember – if you delete the kindle book, the audible book will automatically delete at the same time.

If you have only the Audible book, then the word "Audible" will display to the right of the book name when in List view. An Audible banner will appear at the bottom of the cover when in Grid view.

You can also filter to only see Audible books at all.

You can download an Audible book with a companion Kindle book. Open the Kindle book and then tap the top of the screen in the book to bring up the toolbars. Then tap on the headphone icon to switch to the Audible player. Tap the Download button on the Audible cover from the Audible player.

Rent, Lend & Borrow

Borrow Titles from Amazon Prime Reading

Amazon Prime members can borrow books, magazines and more from the Prime Reading catalog. You can read borrowed content on your supported Fire tablet, Kindle e-reader or Kindle reading app.

Prime Reading allows Amazon Prime members to search and borrow selected content including popular books, magazines, comics and Kindle Singles. Titles available for borrowing are added and removed periodically.

Note: Prime Reading is only available for residents of the U.S.

Unlike the Kindle Owners' Lending Library, Prime Reading doesn't require a Fire or Kindle device. You can use any Kindle e-reader, Fire tablet or Kindle reading apps for iOS, Android or Samsung to read Prime Reading titles.

Kindle for iOS, Kindle for Android, Kindle for Samsung, Fire tablet and Kindle e-readers all support Prime Reading content such as books, comics and Kindle Singles. Use your browser to visit Kindle store to access the Prime Reading catalog for other devices.

Desktop browsers, Kindle for iOS, Kindle for Android, Kindle for Samsung and Fire tablets support browsing for Prime Reading magazines. Browsing for Prime Reading magazines is yet not available from the Kindle Store for Kindle e-reader devices. Use the experimental web browser to borrow Prime Reading magazines from Kindle e-readers by locating the magazine title on the Amazon website.

Note: You cannot read magazines from the Prime Reading catalog on Kindle Cloud Reader, Kindle for PC or Kindle for Mac.

Borrow a Title from Prime Reading

Follow these steps to borrow a title using your Prime Reading benefits:

1. Access the Prime Reading Catalog by visiting https://www.amazon.com/primereading.
2. View the product detail page of the title that you wish to borrow.
3. Select the option to borrow the title for free with Prime Reading. Then select the device or Kindle reading app you will be using to read the borrowed title.

   Tip: It's also possible to borrow the title for free with Prime Reading through the Kindle Store using the Kindle app for iOS or Android as well as Kindle e-readers and Fire tablets.

If you cancel your Amazon Prime membership or it expires you will lose access to a borrowed title.

Return a Title Borrowed from Prime Reading

Titles you borrow can be returned at any time as there are no due dates .

Follow these steps to return a title that you have borrowed:

1. Go to Manage Your Content and Devices (https://www.amazon.com/mycd).
2. Find the title you wish to return.
3. Click the **Actions** button next to the title. Then select **Return this title**.
4. Click **Yes** to confirm.

Borrow Books from the Kindle Owner's Lending Library

If you are an Amazon Prime member you can borrow books from the Kindle Owners' Lending Library and read them on your Kindle e-reader, Fire tablet or Fire phone.

Amazon Prime members with paid Amazon Prime, paid Prime Student, 30-day free trial and customers receiving a free month of Prime benefits with a Fire tablet and who own a Kindle e-reader, Fire tablet or Fire phone can enjoy reading the thousands of titles that Kindle Owners' Lending Library offers. There are no due dates for the book borrowed from the Kindle Owners' Lending Library. Borrowed books can be downloaded from the Cloud to other devices such as Kindle e-readers, Fire tablets and Fire phones registered to the same Amazon account.

62

Note:

- You cannot read borrowed books on Kindle reading apps.
- Prime Student Trial Membership does not include access to Kindle Owners' Lending Library. Users who were invited to share only shipping benefits with a Prime Member are also denied access.
- You can share titles borrowed from Kindle Owners' Lending Library with another adult in your household through Amazon Household and Family Library with select Prime memberships.

Borrow a Book from Kindle Owners' Lending Library

Prime Members are allowed to borrow one book per calendar month from the Kindle Owners' Lending Library. A borrowed book can be downloaded to compatible devices registered under the same Amazon Household account. Titles that are available are subject to regular change.

Note: You will see 'Monthly limit reached' text under the **Borrow for Free** button in the Kindle Store if you have already borrowed a book from Kindle Owners' Lending Library for the current month. The text 'Prime members only' will appear underneath the **Borrow for Free** button once you're eligible to borrow again.

Follow these steps to borrow a book:

1. Open the Kindle Store from your device.
2. Locate a title that is eligible to borrow.
3. Select **Borrow for Free**. You will be prompted to return any remaining borrowed titles before borrowing a new title.

You will lose access to a borrowed title if you cancel your Amazon Prime membership or if your Amazon Prime Membership expires.

Return a Book Borrowed from Kindle Owners' Lending Library

You can return books borrowed from the Kindle Owners' Lending Library any time as they have no due dates. The bookmarks, notes and highlights that you add to the book will be saved to your Amazon account. They will be available if you borrow or buy the same book at a later date.

Follow these steps to return a book:

1. Go to Manage Your Content and Devices (https://www.amazon.com/mycd). Then go to the **Your Content** tab.
2. Select the **Actions** button next to the book you wish to return.
3. Select **Return this book**. Then select **Yes** in the pop-up window that appears.

Borrow Books from a Public Library

There are more than 11,000 libraries in the U.S. which offer Public Library Books for Kindle. Check out available Kindle books by visiting the website of your local library and have books sent directly to your Fire tablet, Kindle device or Kindle reading app.

Kindle books borrowed from a public library are available to you only for a specific period of time; similar to physical library books. Many libraries throughout the United States offer public library books for Kindle. OverDrive is the digital service that provides public library books.

Note: Public Library books for Kindle are only available in Kindle format.

Check Out a Public Library Book

Follow these steps to browse public library books for Kindle:

1. Go to Overdrive (https://www.overdrive.com/) or to the website of your local library and confirm that your library branch is eligible and carries Kindle books.
2. Obtain a PIN and a library card from your local library.
3. Go to the website of your local public library and search for Kindle books / eBooks.
4. Sign in to your Amazon account at checkout and select the Fire tablet, Kindle e-reader or the supported Kindle reading app to send the book to.
5. Connect your device to Wi-Fi. Download the title from the Archived Items or Cloud.
   Tip: Sync your device manually if you do not receive the book.

Restrictions:

- Depending on the library, availability of books and length of loan will vary.

- You must be connected to a Wi-Fi network to have Public library books delivered to a Kindle e-reader. Public library books cannot be delivered via 3G connections.
- Some titles may have publisher restrictions that require them to be transferred wirelessly from your computer using the USB cable. You cannot access restricted titles on Kindle reading apps.

Return a Library Book

Go to Manage Your Content and Devices (https://www.amazon.com/mycd) to return a library book before the loan period ends.

Always check with your public library about the due date of a borrowed book since the length of a book loan is determined by each individual library. Amazon sends you a courtesy reminder, three days before the book is due and another email notification when the loan period has ended.

Follow these steps to return a library book:

1. Go to Manage Your Content and Devices (https://www.amazon.com/mycd).
2. Select the **Actions** button next to the book that you wish to return from **Your Content**.
3. Select **Return This Book**. Then select **Yes** in the pop-up window that appears.

Once a book is returned, you will no longer have access to it. Any saved notes and highlights can be accessed through Manage Your Content and Devices (https://www.amazon.com/mycd) even after returning a book. Your notes and highlights will appear in the book if you check out or purchase the book from Amazon at a later date.

Lend or Borrow Kindle Books

It's possible to lend a Kindle book to another reader for up to 14 days. The borrower is not required to own a Fire tablet or Kindle e-reader and can use a free Kindle reading app to read the book after downloading it.

You can only lend a Kindle book once. Currently, it's not possible to lend magazines and newspapers.

Loan a Kindle Book from the Product Detail Page

If a Kindle book is eligible to be loaned, you can loan it from the product detail page of the book. You will not have access to the book during the loan period.

Follow these steps to loan a Kindle book:

1. Locate the book you wish to loan by going to the Kindle Store (https://www.amazon.com/gp/browse.html?node=133141011) from your computer.
2. Click **Loan this book** on the product detail page. You will then be redirected to the **Loan this book** page.
3. You can enter the recipient's email address as well as an optional message.
   Note: Ensure that you send the Kindle book loan notification to the personal email address of the recipient instead of their Kindle email address.

4. Click **Send now**.
   Note: If the book is not accepted by the recipient within seven days, it will reappear in your content library where you will be able to loan it again if you wish to.

Loan a Kindle Book from Manage Your Content and Devices

An eligible Kindle book can be loaned from the product detail page. You will not be able to access the book that you loan during the loan period.

Follow these steps to loan a book:

1. Go to Manage Your Content and Devices (https://www.amazon.com/mycd).
2. Select the **Actions** button for the title that you want to loan. Then select **Loan this title**. If the option **Loan this title** is not present, lending is not available for that particular title.
3. You can enter the recipient's email address as well as an optional message.
   Note: Ensure that you send the Kindle book loan notification to the personal email address of the recipient instead of their Kindle email address.

4.   Click **Send now**.

Borrow from a Friend

When a friend has loaned you a Kindle book, you will be notified by an email. You can download the book to your Fire tablet, Kindle e-reader or supported Kindle reading app through the email.

Follow these steps to download a borrowed book:

1.   Open the email notification 'A Loaned Book for You.'
2.   Click the **Get your loaned book now** button. You will be automatically redirected to Amazon where you can accept the loan.
3.   Sign in to your Amazon account.
     • Fire tablet, Kindle e-reader or Kindle reading app users must select the device they would like the book to be delivered to and click **Accept loaned book**.
     • Use a free Kindle reading app if you do not have a Fire tablet, Kindle e-reader or Kindle reading app by clicking **Accept loaned book** and following the on-screen instructions to download a free Kindle reading app.

Return a Loaned Book

Follow these steps to return a loaned Kindle book:

1.   Go to Manage Your Content and Devices (https://www.amazon.com/mycd).
2.   Select the **Actions [...]** button next to the borrowed book. Then select **Delete from library**.
3.   Confirm by clicking **Yes**.

Rent Kindle Textbooks

You can rent Kindle textbooks for a fixed or flexible rental period. You can choose the length of the rental period with flexible rentals and specify the exact number of days you need. You may purchase a Kindle textbook or choose to have the rental period extended if needed.

You are still able access your saved notes and highlights after your rental period is over. Your previously saved notes and highlights will reappear if you re-rent or purchase the title in the future.

Extend Your Kindle Textbook Rental

Extending your rental period any time prior to its expiration is easy if your rental is flexible.

Note: It's possible to re-rent a Kindle textbook once your rental period expires. It will be treated as a new rental period.

Follow these steps to extend the duration of a Kindle textbook rental:

1. Go to Manage Your Content and Devices (https://www.amazon.com/mycd).
2. Select your rented textbook. Then click **Extend or Purchase** from the **Actions** drop-down menu.
3. Enter the new end date for your rental. Review the cost for the additional rental period.
4. Pay the additional cost and extend your rental period by following onscreen directions.

Purchase Your Kindle Textbook Rental

If you purchase a Kindle textbook that has been rented before the expiration of the rental period, you will only be required to pay the difference in price between the purchase price and what you have already paid in rental costs.

Follow these steps to purchase a Kindle textbook rental:

1. Go to Manage Your Content and Devices (https://www.amazon.com/mycd).
2. Select your rented textbook. Click **Extend or Purchase** from the **Actions** drop-down menu.
3. Select **Buy now.** Pay the additional cost to purchase the title by following the onscreen instructions. Note: the rental credit will be applied against the full cost of the textbook before completing the purchase.

You will have to purchase your Kindle textbook at full price if you no longer have the option to apply your rental credit to the purchase price.

Return Kindle Books

You may be able to return books and comics that you bought from the Kindle Store for a refund. Amazon will consider your return. Your request should be received by Amazon within seven days of purchase.

Here are the steps to return an eligible Kindle book:

1. Go to Manage Your Content and Devices (https://www.amazon.com/mycd).
2. From the **Your Content** tab select the **Actions [...]** button next to the title that you want to return. After that you need to select **Return for Refund**.
3. Select **Return for Refund** in the pop-up box.

Tip: Accidentally purchased using Kindle? You can cancel a Kindle book order immediately after purchase. Select the "Purchased by Accident? Cancel this Order" tab immediately after you purchased a book on your device.

Prevent accidental purchases by turning on the parental controls on your Kindle e-reader. After starting parental controls, you can restrict access to the Kindle Store, Amazon Appstore and more.

Return Kindle Books Purchased for Others

If you purchased multiple Kindle books for others, you may be able to return the unredeemed portion of the order for a refund within 60 days of purchase.

Here is the process to request to return all unredeemed copies in the order.

1. Go to Your Digital Orders (https://www.amazon.com/yourdigitalorders).
2. Locate your order and click "Return unredeemed books".
3. Select your reason for return and click "Submit".

Refunds are issued using the same payment method used for the original purchase and it usually completed within 3-5 business days.

Note: Returns are not available on single-copy orders sent as a gift.

Kindle Content as Gifts

Purchase a Kindle Book as a Gift

You can now send or receive Kindle books as gifts even if you do not own an Amazon device. Recipients can read a Kindle book gift on a supported Amazon device or Kindle reading app. Before purchasing a Kindle book as a gift, make sure that the recipient's email address is valid.

Note: you will need a valid 1-Click payment method linked to your account in order to gift a Kindle book title. You can set this up by going to Manage Your Content and Devices (https://www.amazon.com/mycd). Once completed, select the **Settings** tab and then click **Edit Payment Method** below **Digital Payment Settings**.

Here are some steps to purchase a Kindle book as a gift:

Select the book that you want to purchase as a gift from the Kindle Store (https://www.amazon.com/gp/browse.html?node=133141011) in your desktop browser.

Note: Free books, books on pre-order, and subscriptions cannot be gifted at this time.

1. Click the **Buy for others** button from the product detail page.
2. Enter the personal email address of your gift recipient.
   a. **Tip:** If you are unsure of the recipient's e-mail address, you can select **Email the gift to me** before placing your order. Then, you can forward the gift email or print and personally deliver it to your recipient. The recipient will need to enter the **Gift Claim Code** from the email after logging in to their Amazon account.
3. Enter a delivery date and an optional gift message.
4. Click **Place your order** to finish your gift purchase using your Amazon 1-Click payment method.

You can redeliver a Kindle book gift that you've purchased by going to Your Digital Orders in Your Account. Simply click the **Resend E-mail** button from the Order Summary page.

Country and copyright restrictions may limit the availability of Titles. If a gifted title isn't available for your gift recipient, they can contact Amazon support and Amazon will exchange your gift for an equivalent value with Amazon.com Gift Card.

Redeem a Kindle Book Gift

If you do not own a Fire tablet or Kindle e-reader, you can still receive Kindle books as gifts. Without having a supported Amazon device which is registered to your account; download a free Kindle reading app after you accept your gift.

Here is the step to redeem a Kindle book gift:

1. Click **Get your Kindle Book Gift Now** from the gift notification email to view your gift on Amazon.
2. Click **accept your Kindle Book Gift**. After that it will be prompted to log in to your Amazon account.
3. **Tip:** Once you've received a Kindle book gift at an email address that is not associated with your Fire tablet, Kindle e-reader, or Kindle reading app, you will need to click **Use a different Amazon account** and sign in to the account where you would like to redeem your Kindle book.

4. Select the Fire tablet, Kindle device or Kindle reading app that you would like the gift delivered to from the drop-down menu.

Note: If you live in a different country to the person who gave you the Kindle book gift, the book may not be available to you due to copyright restrictions. In this case, you will be given the option to request an exchange for an Amazon.com Gift Card on your account during the redemption process.

Exchange a Kindle Book Gift for an Amazon.com Gift Card

You can exchange the Kindle book gift for an Amazon.com Gift Card, redeemable on millions of other items on Amazon; including other Kindle books.

Here are the steps to exchange a Kindle book gift for an Amazon.com Gift Card:

1. Open the gift email that you received and then select **Get your Kindle book gift now**.
2. Select **Learn how this works or exchange for gift credit** from the **Accept your Kindle Book Gift** page.
3. Select **Request your gift credit from customer service now** from the following screen.

You will receive a confirmation e-mail and an Amazon.com Gift Card applied to your registered account equal to the current price of the Kindle book.

Share What You're Reading

Find and Share Books with Goodreads on Kindle

Goodreads on Kindle makes it easy for you to connect with the Goodreads community and follow friends to see what they are reading and share and rate books on your Kindle. You can shop directly through Goodreads for Kindle books and selected titles.

With Goodreads on Kindle you will be connected to the world's largest community of readers. Find personalized book recommendations, review your reading history, keep track of what you want to read in the future and see and discuss what your friends are reading.

Get started by tapping the Goodreads icon on the toolbar where you will be prompted to sign in to Goodreads or create a new account if you do not already have one.

You can search for and add Facebook friends when you create a new account. Any Facebook friends who already use Goodreads will automatically be added to your Goodreads friend list when you sign-in using your Facebook account. The more friends and readers you follow on Goodreads, the more recommendations you will see.

When you log in to an existing Goodreads account, your account data, such as your friends list, your Want to Read list, Currently Read and Read shelves, will synchronize with your browser. Add books to your Goodreads shelves to track what you read. When you set up your account, you will be sent a list of your digital and physical Amazon book purchases.

You can rate books from one to five stars. When you rate a book, it is added to your Read shelf. You can shelve a book as Currently Reading or Want to Read by tapping the Shelf icon. Your shelved and rated books will appear on your public profile in Goodreads.

72

Tap the **Shelf** icon and select **Remove** from Shelf to remove a shelved book. You can also add books to your Goodreads shelves from the **Home** screen of your Kindle Paperwhite by tapping the **Menu** icon on the item's cover when in grid view or by tapping the right side of the screen in list view. Then tap **Add** to Goodreads Shelf. Use a shortcut by pressing and holding on the book's name or cover. Then select a shelf from Read, Currently Reading or Want to Read from the Select Goodreads Shelf pane.

In order to use Goodreads on Kindle, your Kindle must be registered with your Amazon account and connected to Wi-Fi. Your Kindle needs to be registered with the Amazon account you want to connect to Goodreads. Goodreads can only be accessed by customers in the United States, Canada, Australia and international customers who are registered with an Amazon account.

Follow these steps to connect your Amazon account to Goodreads:

1. Tap the **Goodreads** g icon in the toolbar from **Home**.
2. Completing one of the following options:
   - **If you already have a Goodreads account:** Tap **Already a Goodreads Member?** and enter your Goodreads login information. Enter your Facebook login information if your Goodreads account is linked to your Facebook account. It's also possible to enter by simply tapping **Sign In with Facebook**.
   - **If you don't already have a Goodreads account:** Create a new Goodreads account with your Amazon login information by tapping **Activate Goodreads**.
3. Start receiving personalized recommendations by picking a few genres and rating a books that you have read. Proceed through the screens by tapping **Next**.
   Note: A book is automatically added to your **Read** shelf (if it's already not there) when you rate it.

4. You can connect your Goodreads account to Facebook by entering your Facebook login information. Tap **Next**. You can **Skip** this step if you wish to.

Once you connect your Amazon account to Goodreads, your Goodreads profile will be available with your shelves, friends, recommendations and recent updates.

Tips:

- When you come across a book that interests you, tap Want to Read to add it to the shelf. You can also mark a book as Read, Currently Reading or Want to Read by tapping the Shelf icon.
- Tap the stars from one to five to rate a book.
- Read reviews to purchase titles with 1-Click and view book details in the Kindle Store by tapping on a book cover.
- View personalized book recommendations by searching for your friends and approving friend requests.

Share Kindle E-Reader Notes & Highlights

Share your notes and highlights with your friends and social network connections once you have linked your Kindle to Goodreads, Facebook or Twitter.

Follow these steps to share a note or a highlight:

1. Select the highlight or the note that you wish to share.
   - **Highlights**: Highlight the word or passage you wish to share by press and holding the word or press and dragging.
   - **Notes**: Press and hold the number icon for the note you want to share.
2. Tap **Share**.
3. **Optional:** You can include an optional message to send with your shared highlight or note.
4. You can post your note or highlight to your linked Goodreads, Facebook and/or Twitter account/s by tapping **Share**.

   Note: Notes and highlights are shared with Goodreads by default if you have linked your Amazon account to Goodreads. Share on Facebook and Twitter by tapping the checkbox next to their icons In the **Share** window.

Using the Experimental Web Browser

The experimental web browser on your Kindle enables you to browse the web and interact with Amazon web pages. The Experimental Web Browser supports JavaScript, SSL and cookies. Media plug-ins are not supported. A Wi-Fi connection is necessary to access most websites.

Start the Experimental Web Browser by tapping the Home screen Menu icon and then clicking Experimental Browser. A list of default bookmarks will be listed when you first launch the experimental browser and can be later accessed by selecting the Bookmark tab from the web browser menu. Enter a URL in the search field at the top of the screen using the in-built keyboard. A '.com' key is available on the keyboard for your convenience. The last URL you entered in the address field will remain until you type a new URL.

Tips:

• Zoom in on a web page or image by placing two fingers together at the center of the screen and moving them apart. Zoom out by reversing the action.

• Tap links to open a web page.

• Navigate on a web page by dragging your finger left/right and up/down.

• Return to the previous page you were viewing by tapping the Back icon in the upper left corner.

• Drag your finger up the screen to scroll down a web page.

• When entering information on a web page, tap the field and the onscreen keyboard will display.

• Tap the Menu icon and select history to return to previously viewed web pages.

Web browser menu

By clicking the Menu icon within the experimental browser, you can view other options such as Article Mode, Bookmarks, Bookmark this Page, History and Browser Settings. Clear History, Clear Cookies, Disable JavaScript and Disable Images are included in Browser Settings.

Web pages will load faster if JavaScript is disabled. Switching to Article Mode when reading an article will alter the layout of the page and displays the article in simple column text, eliminating surrounding images and advertisements.

Bookmarks

Bookmark a web page by tapping the Menu icon and selecting Bookmark this Page. To delete a bookmark, tap the Menu icon and select Bookmarks, then tap the Remove button at the bottom of the page and then tap and select the URL(s) you want to remove using the checkboxes next to them. Tap the remove button again.

Downloading files

You will be asked to confirm if you want to download content from web pages to read on your Kindle. The items downloaded are added to the home screen. The following file types can be downloaded: Kindle content (.AZW,.AZW1,.AZW3, and.KFX), unprotected Mobipocket books (.MOBI,.PRC), and text files (.TXT).

Troubleshooting

Restart Your Kindle

Restart your device to resolve frozen screen problems or issues with downloading content.

Follow these steps to restart your Kindle:

1. Launch the Power Dialog Box by pressing and holding the **Power** button for seven seconds.
2. Tap **Restart**.
   Note: Press and hold the **power** button for a full 40 seconds in order to restart your device if the Power Dialog Box does not appear.

Storage space

Follow these steps in order to see remaining free storage space on your Kindle:

1. Tap the Quick Actions icon on the toolbar. Then tap All Settings.

2. On the Settings page, tap the Menu icon. Then Device Info.

Slow or Frozen Kindle E-Reader

Restart your Kindle e-reader or try the troubleshooting steps below if your device screen is slow to respond or freezes.

Troubleshooting Frozen Screen

Press and hold or slide and hold the **Power** button for a full 40 seconds. Make sure that you do this for 40 seconds, even after the screen goes blank before letting go. If the device does not start up on its own, press or slide the **Power** button.

Plug in your device using the USB code or a power adapter if the screen is still unresponsive. It's recommended that Kindle are charged with an Amazon power adapter. Try to restart again after charging the device for 30 minutes.

Troubleshooting Slow Screen Response

At times you might experience a slow or unresponsive Kindle e-reader screen. Optimize the screen performance of your device by following the troubleshooting steps.

Potential Issue	Troubleshooting Steps
Restart needed	In order to Restart, your device must turn off completely and then restarted. Restart your device from the Power dialog or Settings menu: • Select **Menu** from **Home**. Then select **Settings**. From **Settings**, select **Menu** again and then select **Restart**.
Previous software version	Check whether your device has the latest software version. Go to Fire & Kindle Software Updates (https://www.amazon.com/gp/help/customer/display.html?nodeId=200529680) and select your device to find the latest software update.

Potential Issue	Troubleshooting Steps
Download in progress	You might experience a slow response time if you are currently downloading content on your device. Your device may also respond slowly immediately after downloading a large amount of content.
Device temperature	Avoid using your device in extreme hot or cold surroundings.
Device accessories	Try removing any protective cases or screens and test the performance of the device without them.
Touchscreen is dirty	Use a soft, slightly damp, lint-free cloth to clean the screen. Do not use the device while wearing gloves, with wet hands or immediately after applying hand lotion.
Low battery	Charge your battery for at least 30 minutes and then try restarting again.
Reset needed	Try resetting your device if you continue to experience slowness after restarting your device. **Important:** Note that resetting your device will remove your personal information (including your settings for Parental Controls), Amazon account information, Wi-Fi settings and any downloaded content. A factory reset will remove all content you have downloaded to your device. Make sure that you back-up your content to your computer before resetting your device. Content that you purchased from Amazon can be downloaded again when you register your Fire tablet or Kindle e-reader to your account as it is automatically saved to the Cloud.

Potential Issue	Troubleshooting Steps

You may lose any in-app items on your Kindle e-reader during a factory reset. Before completing a factory reset, check with the app developer for more details on their in-app policies.

Select **Menu** from the **Home** screen. Then select **Settings**. Select **Menu** again and select **Reset Device** or **Reset to Factory Defaults**.

Kindle E-Reader Won't Stay Charged

If your Kindle takes longer than six hours to fully charge or has trouble maintaining charge, follow these troubleshooting steps.

When using a power adapter, ensure the USB cable is securely connected. Faulty or damaged USB cables and power adapters cause battery charging issues.

Follow these steps to conserve battery life:

- **Put your Kindle into sleep mode when you have finished reading.** Conserve battery live by pressing the **Power** button to put your Kindle into sleep mode. Close the cover to put your device into sleep mode if it's a Kindle Paperwhite (8th Generation).
- **Turn off your wireless connection.** Wi-fi or 3g connection can consume extra battery power. Disable your wireless connections by tapping the **Quick Actions** icon and then tapping **Airplane Mode**.
- **Use a compatible power adapter for charging.** Always charge your Kindle with the supplied USB cable. **Note**: Some computers and older keyboards may not provide the required power to fully charge the device. Your Kindle should fully charge in less than six hours with a compatible power adapter (sold separately).

- **Restart your Kindle.** Disconnect your Kindle device from the USB cable. Press and hold the **power** button for 7 seconds to launch the Power Dialog Box. In the Power Dialog Box, tap **Restart**. Connect the USB cable to your Kindle and your computer or a compatible power adapter to ensure the Kindle charges.
- **Charge Kindle Paperwhite with the cover.** Kindle Paperwhite Leather Charging cover has a battery that provides extra battery life when paired with Kindle Paperwhite (8th Generation). When paired together and connected to a power source both Kindle Paperwhite (8th Generation) and Kindle Paperwhite Leather Charging Cover should charge fully.

Content Won't Download to Your Kindle E-Reader

If you do not see a downloaded title listed on your Home screen, follow these steps.

1. **Sync to receive your content.** Tap the **Quick Actions** icon from **Home** screen. Then tap **Sync My Kindle**.
2. **Restart Your Kindle.** Launch the Power Dialog Box by pressing and holding the power button for **7 seconds**. Then tap **Restart**.

Note: Press and hold the **Power** button for a full **40 seconds** if the Power dialog box doesn't appear.

3. **Check your wireless connection.** View the wireless indicators from the **Home** or any **Settings** screen. Tap the top of the screen to view the status indicators while reading.
4. **Check your software version.** Update your Kindle device to the latest available software version.
5. **Check if your payment method is valid.** Check the validity of your 1-Click payment settings.
6. **Check if you are filtering content.** Tap **My Library** from **Home** and then tap the **Downloaded** tab. The name of the left drop-down menu in the upper right corner of the screen will appear as **Books**, **Periodicals**, **Docs** or **Collections**(for compatible devices) if you are not viewing all items. Tap **All Items** to view **All** items.
7. **Restart your Kindle.** Launch the Power Dialog Box by pressing and holding the power button for **7 seconds.** Then tap **Restart**.

Can't Connect to Wi-Fi

Follow these troubleshooting steps if you cannot connect to Wi-Fi.

- **Check your Device's Wireless Connectivity.** Your Kindle will not connect to 3G (if applicable) or to a Wi-Fi network that you have used before if Wireless Connectivity is enabled on your device.
- **Use Channel 1-11.** Check whether your wireless router is set to use a Wi-Fi channel between 1 to 11. For additional help, refer to your internet service provider or the router manufacturer.
- **Restart your Kindle and modem and/or router.** Launch the Power Dialog Box by pressing and holding the power button for **7 seconds.** Then tap **Screen Off**. Turn off your router and/or modem for 30 seconds. Then turn them back on. Press and hold the **power** button on your Kindle until it turns on once your router and/or modem restarts. Try to connecting to your Wi-Fi network again.

If you are still having trouble connecting, there may be an issue with your network hardware or your Internet connection. Contact your internet service provider for further troubleshooting.

Can't Find Wi-Fi Password to Register Amazon Device

You may need to connect your Kindle to a wireless network in order to set up and register your Amazon device.

To connect your Kindle e-reader, Fire tablet, Fire phone or Fire TV to a wireless network, you must first know the name of the Wi-Fi network and the password for the network (if required).

Tip: In some instances your network name may be referred to as an **SSID**. Your password may be referred to as a **passphrase** or a **key**.

Follow these steps to find your network name or password:

- Check the sticker located on the bottom of your router.
- Check your router's installation guide or the owner's manual.
- View the wireless settings on a device such as a Windows PC, Mac or mobile phone that is already connected to your network.

Windows PC

Follow these steps to view the wireless settings on most Windows PCs:

1. Left-click the wireless icon in the taskbar.

    Tip: Switch to **Desktop** mode. Then left-click the wireless icon on Windows .

2. Right-click the name of the **Connected** network. Then click **Properties**.
3. Your network name should be listed under **Name** or **SSID** on the **Connection** tab.
4. Your password should be listed next to **Network security key** on the **Security** tab.

    Note: You must be logged in as Administrator in order to show your password.

Contact your internet service provider or the person who helped set up your wireless network if you are still unable to locate your network name or password.

Mac OS X

Follow these steps to view the wireless settings on most Mac devices running OS X:

1. Open the **Utilities** folder. Then open the **Keychain Access** app.
2. Click your wireless network name. Then click the **info** button.
3. Check the box next to **Show Password**.

    Note: You will need to enter the administrator password for your device to show your password.

Contact your internet service provider or the person who helped set up your wireless network if you are still unable to locate your network name or password.

Book Won't Open on Kindle E-Reader

Follow these troubleshooting steps if your book won't open on your Kindle or if there is an error when you try to open a book.

Follow these steps to download the book again:

1. Ensure your Kindle device is connected to a wireless network.
2. Tap **My Library** from **Home.** Then tap the **Downloaded** tab.
3. Press and hold the title of the Kindle book you wish to delete. Tap **Delete This Book**.

4. Tap the **Menu** ⋮ icon. Then tap **Settings**. Tap the **Menu** icon again and then tap **Restart**.

5. Once your Kindle device restarts, tap the **All** tab. Then click the title of the Kindle book you wish to start downloading.

Content Won't Sync on Your Kindle E-Reader

Synchronization might be disabled on your Kindle device or Amazon account or you may not be connected to a wireless network if your notes, highlights, furthest page read and collections fail to sync across your devices or Kindle reading apps.

Follow these steps to sync your Kindle content:

1. **Ensure that Whispersync for Books is enabled on your Kindle device.** Tap the **Menu** ⋮ **icon** from **Home** screen. Click **Settings** and then **Device Options**. Select **Advanced Options**. If **Whispersync for Books** is **Not Enabled**, tap this option and select **Enable**.

2. **Ensure that Whispersync Device Synchronization is enabled on your Amazon account.** Go to Manage Your Content and Devices (https://www.amazon.com/mycd) from your computer and select **Settings**. Under **Device Synchronization (Whispersync Settings)**, verify that **Whispersync Device Synchronization** is turned **ON**.

3. **Check the status of your wireless connection.** View the wireless indicators from **Home** or **Settings** screen. Tap the top of the screen while reading to view the indicators.

4. **Check your software version.** Update your device to the latest available software version.

5. **Manually sync your device.** Tap the top of the screen while reading to view the reading toolbar. Then tap the **Quick Actions** icon and then tap **Sync My Kindle**.

Reset Your Kindle

Resetting your device will remove all downloaded content and you will be required to register the device again.

Important: All personal information such as your lock screen passcode and parental controls, Amazon account information, Wi-Fi settings and downloaded content will be removed when resetting your Kindle device. You can download any content purchased from Amazon that has been saved to the Cloud when you link your Kindle to your account again. It is recommended that you **Restart Your Kindle** without removing personal information or settings if you are having trouble with your device.

Make sure that you transfer any content that is not saved in the Cloud from your device to your computer via USB before resetting your Kindle.

If you would like to reset your Kindle but have forgotten your parental controls password, enter **111222777** as the parental controls password.

Follow these steps to *reset your Kindle*:

1. Tap the **Menu** ⋮ icon from **Home**. Then tap **Settings**.
2. Tap the **Menu** icon again and then tap **Reset Device**. Your Kindle will now restart.

You will need to connect your Kindle to a wireless network and register it before using it again.

Water Protection

Your Kindle has been tested to withstand brief accidental immersion in water under critical conditions, however, your Kindle is NOT intended for underwater use. If your kindle does come into contact with water, it may experience some damage. Follow these instructions below for your Kindle:

• Quickly retrieve your Kindle. If your Kindle has a cover, remove the cover immediately. • If your Kindle was immersed in fresh water, immediately unplug all cables. Drain your Kindle by standing it stand upright with the micro-USB port facing down. • If your Kindle has been immersed in other types of water, unplug all cables, drain your Kindle by letting it stand upright with the micro-USB port facing down, rinse your Kindle using fresh water (such as cold tap water) with the micro-USB port facing the water source and drain your Kindle again. • Leave the device to fully dry in a well-ventilated location before plugging the USB cable into your Kindle. • Do not to attempt to dry your Kindle with an external heat source (such as a microwave oven or hair dryer). • Do not insert a foreign object into the micro-USB port (such as a cotton swab or paper towel).

To reduce the risk of damage to your Kindle, follow these instructions:

• Do not intentionally immerse your Kindle in water or expose it to seawater, salt water, chlorinated water or other liquids (such as beverages). • Do not spill any food, oil, lotion, or other abrasive substances on your Kindle. • Never expose your Kindle to pressurized water, high velocity water, or extremely humid conditions (such as a steam room).

www.ingramcontent.com/pod-product-compliance
Lightning Source LLC
LaVergne TN
LVHW041217050326
832903LV00021B/674